S0-BWH-501

KAZUYOSHI NOMACHI

A PHOTOGRAPHER'S
PILGRIMAGE
[30 years of great reportage]

TEXT AND PHOTOGRAPHS
by KAZUYOSHI NOMACHI

EDITORIAL DIRECTOR

VALERIA MANFERTO DE FABIANIS

GRAPHIC DESIGN

CLARA ZANOTTI

VMB Publishers®
An imprint of White Star S.p.A., Italy

© 2005 White Star S.p.A.
Via Candido Sassone, 22/24
13100 Vercelli, Italy - www.whitestar.it
TRANSLATION: Michael Hoffman

All rights reserved. No part of this publication may be reproduced, stored in a retrieval system
or transmitted in any form or by any means, electronic, mechanical, photocopying, recording or
otherwise, without written permission from the publisher. Vmb Publishers® is a registered
trademark property of White Star s.p.a.

ISBN 13: 978-88-540-0596-9.

REPRINTS:
1 2 3 4 5 6 11 10 09 08 07

Printed in China
Color separation by Chiaroscuro, Turin

4

1 A deacon reads his
Bible in a grotto
church in the holy city
of Lalibela, Ethiopia.

2-3 A Tibetan
Buddhist nun, rosary
entwined round her
fingers, makes the
Mandala offering.

5 A group of women
pilgrims from Kerala
State in southern India
take part in the *hajj*

INTRODUCTION

I T WAS APRIL 1973, AS I RECALL. I WAS STAYING AT A SMALL OASIS IN WESTERN ALGERIA. IT WAS MY SECOND TRIP TO THE SAHARA. JUST OUTSIDE THE OASIS WAS A HILL OF SAND SOME 165 FT (50 M) HIGH. FROM THE TOP OF THE HILL ONE LOOKED OUT ONTO A MAJESTIC SEA OF SAND EXTENDING AS FAR AS THE EYE COULD SEE.

One day toward evening, when the sinking of the blazing sun afforded a measure of relief from the heat, I climbed the hill to take some pictures. With me was a sixteen-year-old boy with whom I'd become friendly. The sandy expanse glowed pink in the setting sun, the evening tints changing from minute to minute. When at last I looked up from my camera, the boy was gone. We had been laughing and kidding each other on the way here. Where could he have disappeared to?

There he was on the other side of the hill, deep in his evening prayers. Facing east, he bowed deeply, kneeled, prostrated himself, then rose to his feet, praying all the while. I was somewhat taken aback. A few moments before he'd been an ordinary teenage boy, almost a child. Now all trace of childishness was gone. He was a man – dignified, resolute man of the desert, face to face with his God.

Taking no notice of me, though I stood right beside him in the advancing dusk, he was the very image of a man lost in prayer. He was as though entranced. His repeated prostrations had left his face, from his forehead to his shapely nose, caked with grains of golden sand. Just at that moment, as he faced east toward Mecca, the moon rose on the eastern horizon, full and brilliant. It was a beautiful sight. Here in the vast desert was a naked soul face to face with God, nothing coming between them. For the first time I felt the awesome spiritual depths of the desert.

It was my fascination with the Sahara that encouraged me to widen my horizons. I roamed the Nile Valley, visited Arabia, then went to Tibet, in each place giving my curiosity free rein. I have been to most of the so-called remote regions of the earth – vast stretches of desert, plateau and savanna where modern civilization does not easily penetrate, where transcendent spirits are worshipped generation after generation by people whose religion – prayer in its most primeval form – is a direct expression of the land that spawned it.

Each religion – Buddhism, Islam, Christianity, animism – has its own form of prayer, channeling the sincere worshipper's fear or gratitude toward nature into direct communion with God or the gods. Prayer thus becomes, over the course of a lifetime, a kind of mental pilgrimage. Many pilgrimage routes exist,

6-7 A million worshippers observe Laylat al-Qadr, praying through the night at Mecca's holy mosque on the 27th day of Ramadan.

8-9 Pilgrims proceed through the pre-dawn darkness to crosses planted in the ice deep in the Andes.

11 A valley oasis veiled in dust clouds. The sandstorm season in the Sahara runs from March to April. °

some abstract, others concrete — physical roads leading to geographical holy sites. Islam, for example, centers on the Kaaba sanctuary in Mecca, symbol of the one God. During the pilgrimage months it draws millions of worshippers, traveling to and from the sacred site over a vast worldwide network. Then there is Lalibela, holy center of Ethiopia's Greek Orthodox faith, where barefoot pilgrims camp out for days, their pilgrimage routes mere mountain footpaths, unchanged since the days of the Bible.

There are pilgrims in Tibet, their faith absolute and unconditional, who spend five years, ten years, even twenty years proceeding at a snail's pace to a sacred site many hundreds of miles distant. Wearing clogs on their hands, they clap their hands over their heads, chant the mantra "Om Mani Padme Hum," then crawl along the ground, rise, advance no farther than the length of their bodies, stop, crawl again, and so on, their faces soaked with sweat and begrimed with dust.

On an almost deserted straight road rising through the highest parts of Tibet I met two women pilgrims proceeding in that manner to the holy city of Lhasa. It was then that I realized that the attainment of faith on this level is the labor of a lifetime. Tibetans believe that the soul, migrating from life to life, must accumulate merit over the course of several lifetimes in order to attain deliverance from worldly attachment. Evil deeds cast the soul down into the realms of beasts and hungry ghosts, where the attainment of merit is impossible. The harsher the penance, Tibetans believe, the purer grows the heart of the penitent.

The average Japanese only occasionally turns his

thoughts to religion. Tibetans, on the other hand, regard faith as the central element of their lives. Once I trained my camera on a face twisted in agony from penance; suddenly as I looked through the viewfinder the face broke into a radiant smile. It was a revelation. It pierced me to the heart.

I find highland cultures and faiths deeply appealing – not only Tibet's but Ethiopia's and those of the Andes as well. The thin mountain air makes for limited vegetation; each highland region develops its own unique food culture, hardy and resistant to cultural incursion from the lowlands. What cultural fusion there is produces new and unexpected forms. Tibetan Buddhists, believers in transmigration, acknowledge the presence among them of more than 1000 "living Buddhas," and accord them unconditional faith. Ethiopian Orthodox Christians worship the Holy Ark they believe they inherited from ancient Judaism. In the Andes, the indigenous religions seeped into and merged with the Catholicism forced upon the native peoples by their Spanish conquerors.

Today, the forces of globalization are busy ironing the rich tapestry of cultural diversity into a flat sheet, a standardized civilization. Only on the isolated mountain heights of the several continents, perhaps, do alternative cultures, buttressed by their overwhelming spirituality, have a chance of survival.

Did God create the world, as the Bible and other traditions teach? Or is God merely an illusion of people who have worn themselves out in prayer? Different religions, different regions, different individuals see the world differently. Having acquired that delicate fragile quality called intelligence, human beings cannot be at ease without entrusting their hearts to the protection of a transcendent being. With due allowance made for individual differences, this is part of our human fate. It is written into our DNA. We walk through life in the company of an unseen Someone, whose presence we may only sense when confusion causes us to stumble and lose our footing.

Lately, whenever I go back to my hometown of Kochi on the island of Shikoku, I am struck by the number of pilgrims making the rounds of the temples there. On their conical pilgrims' hats, worn low over their eyes, are the characters "two going together." Watching them as they walk purposefully along the country roads, I sense in them the earnest search for something they feel they have lost. Am I reading too much into it? Or have our daily lives placed us at too great a distance from the realities of prayer and faith?

The regions of the world I have wandered in over the past thirty years are very different from Japan. They are poor and none too safe; and yet people there cling to each other, their warm mutual feelings a solid bulwark against a harsh environment. Alongside this bulwark is a visible "corridor of prayer." After my encounter with the Sahara in my mid-twenties, I circled the globe, proceeding counterclockwise, finally crossing the Pacific to the Andes of South America. In this manner I have experienced firsthand the world's diversity.

In fall 2003, while two monotheisms blustered and clashed like a family at loggerheads, their quarrel shaking the world, I went to the Buddhist nation of Bhutan in the Himalayas. Everywhere one looks are beautiful terraced fields spread out along the mountain slopes. It was harvest time. The men wore go, the women kira – traditional kimono-like garments. Scythes swinging, they mowed down the rice plants. It might have been a Japanese farming village a century ago. The mowing done, they threshed the grain with stones and let the wind separate the grain from the chaff.

The farm women, husks spilling out of their baskets, whistled softly, as though summoning the wind. In the Himalayan valleys the leaves were just beginning turn red. A little brook made a calm whistling noise as it flowed. Society here is matrilineal. Betrothal is a matter of the man entering a girl's bedroom under cover of night and settling in. This country, I was told, has no custom of a formal wedding ceremony.

I was touched by Bhutan's gentle scenery and the modest demeanor of the Bhutanese people. They made me wonder: Does the relentlessly competitive society now prevalent throughout the world, with its law of the jungle and its exclusive monotheisms, have a future? Will we ever, for the sake of our survival, acquire the wisdom to acknowledge diversity, to recognize that there are different ways of seeing the world?

14-15 Two pilgrims from Ngaba in eastern Tibet proceed at a devotional crawl to sacred Lhasa, 1160 miles (1800 km) away.

16-17 Dinka herdsmen living in the White Nile marsh known as Sudd, in southern Sudan.

THE INTIMACY OF THE DESERT

SAHARA

JOURNEY INTO ANOTHER DIMENSION

SAHARA

JOURNEY INTO ANOTHER DIMENSION

I SLIP OUT OF MY TENT INTO THE PREDAWN DARKNESS. IT'S JUST PAST 4 A.M. MY FLASHLIGHT LIGHTS MY WAY AS, CAMERA AND TRIPOD IN TOW, I CLIMB THE CRAGGY MOUNTAIN UNDER A STAR-STUDDED SKY, THERE TO WAIT FOR DAYBREAK.

It's cold – the characteristic cold of a Sahara winter. The rock I sit on is freezing. Not a sign of life anywhere; the only sound a faint ringing in my ears.

Ten minutes pass. A tinge of color in the east signals the approach of dawn. The stars fade from view. Slowly the sand and rocks emerge from the surrounding darkness, the contours of the scene growing every minute more distinct. Still no sound, no sign of life – not so much as a weed anywhere in sight. You'd think the entire world was composed of nothing but mineral substances. The effect is at once terrible and majestic. Changing the exposure as the sky lightens, varying the angle, I snap photo after photo.

It's December 1993 and I'm deep in the Sahara Desert, in Tassili Ahaggar, the no-man's land that constitutes the border between Algeria and Niger. Even by Saharan standards, the dryness here is extreme. There are no wells. We came, my guide and I, equipped with water from the Tamanrasset Oasis. Our gas tank, too,

we filled to capacity. My guide is an elderly Tuareg tribesman. We have been on the road, driving and camping, for five days.

Thirty minutes after the first light of dawn, a crimson sun rises over the Tassili Ahaggar horizon. The land, bare and forbidding, is a veritable moonscape. The air is crystal clear. I feel the sun's warmth on my back. The setting is sublime, like the beginning of the world at the end of the earth.

It was in 1972 that I first set foot in the Sahara. I was in my mid-twenties, and had just started out the year before as a freelance photographer. The first steps in my career were purely commercial. I had one aim in view – to earn enough to feed myself.

It was the Sahara that turned me into a documentary photographer. My encounter with the Sahara, oddly enough, began in the European Alps, where some friends had invited me on a ski tour. The tour ended, and we were in Paris. There, a friend and I bought a battered jalopy, figuring on driving it to Spain.

In Spain we bought a map and studied it. South of Spain lay North Africa, including the vast Sahara. All you had to do was cross the Strait of Gibraltar separating Europe from Africa; then, you could follow a paved road deep in the desert. We hadn't realized that. The

18 A bride who took part in the engagement Mousem (Festival of the Saints) in Imilchil in the High Atlas.

21 Sand drifts composed of extremely fine particles of spherical quartz formed by abrasion.

Sahara – wasn't that the desert in the movie "Lawrence of Arabia"? It was irresistible. We simply had to go. The next thing we knew, we were Sahara-bound.

We drove south, through eastern Morocco and into Algeria. It grew drier and drier. The naked earth and the blue sky were overwhelming. On our second day in Algeria we found ourselves right in the middle of an absolutely inconceivable sea of sand. Sand blew in the wind. It was chestnut-brown; each grain seemed like a nugget of gold. Beautiful. The sand, the rocks, and the stars in the sky. And suddenly, in the midst of all this emptiness, appeared an oasis, populated, it seemed to us, by prisoners of the sand. Tough people leading tough lives. It was as if we'd slipped into another dimension.

From then on I myself was a captive of this strange land – though it wasn't until the following year that my Sahara travels began in earnest.

On the second day of that first trip, at evening, we arrived at the oasis of Kerzaz in southern Algeria. At a rustic little roadside restaurant we had a meal of grilled meat, which filled us up, but there remained the problem of where to spend the night. Just then a young man came over and, introducing himself as an elementary school teacher, invited us to sleep at his place.

His village was some ten minutes off the main road. The school and the teacher's sleeping quarters were in a sandy place a little apart from the community. Our host was friendly and eager to talk; unfortunately my friend and I knew very little French, and conversation foundered. Giving up, we laid down on the mattresses provided for us and soon fell asleep.

We got up next morning and opened the door; the sun was dazzling. Leaving the house and turning the corner, we came upon an astonishing sight. There before us was a mountain of sand, an overwhelming sand wall.

What s scene! It must have been a good 660 ft high (200 m) high, culminating in an exquisite, undulating curve against the clear sky. Still half asleep, I felt as if I'd stumbled upon a fantastic, giant castle – right in the middle of the schoolyard.

At that moment a goatherd approached from the village with a flock of goats.

I had known, of course, that people lived in desert oases, but I could never have imagined how tightly nature encroaches upon daily life here. What kind of people were these folk? I asked myself in my naive curiosity. What kind of lives unfolded in this surrealistic desert world? One of the friends I'd left behind in Paris had said to me, "The desert? You snap one shot toward the sun, one shot away from the sun, and that's it – you've shot everything there is to shoot." He was wrong. The desert – this new dimension – was anything but boring, and anything but simple.

We pressed on, heading south. The Sahara in February is pleasantness itself, the air cool and clear. Hardly any cars were to be seen, but our road was clearly marked on the map, so there seemed nothing to worry about – although whenever we neared a hill of sand we would break out in a sweat, the driver's hands tensing on the steering wheel, as the wind whipped a sandy blizzard across our path. Every obstacle of this sort, once cleared, gave me a feeling of being drawn ever further into the Sahara's mysterious depths.

The oasis lay like a jewel in a wasteland. The village consisted of earth-walled houses and small farms shaded by date palms. Life is quiet here. It moves to its own slow rhythms. As we approached we noticed a plain, unadorned graveyard. In the center were the graves of village founders and holy men, known as marabouts, their graves dignified by a coating of whitewash. Clustered round them were innumerable grave markers of lesser folk, symbols of the generations upon generations that had been born, had lived and had died in an unbroken chain in this tiny oasis.

The village's lifeline is a single aqueduct fed via a tunnel by an underground water vein beneath a mountain slope. A complex irrigation network channels a water supply to each farm. Five-centimeter concrete ditches, like capillaries, protect the water from evaporation. The thin trickle through the moss-fringed ditch made me aware, not for the first time, that in an oasis, life is water.

I got to know a family living there. The household consisted of an elderly couple, their two sons' wives, and the young couples' children. You could see at a glance that their tiny farm couldn't possibly feed so many people. The elderly couple's two sons had gone to work in a distant town – partly to support the family, and partly also because, as devout Muslims, they felt it incumbent upon them to do everything possible to send their parents on a pilgrimage to Mecca. All their lives the old couple had been longing to go.

Five years later I visited the family again. The years had left their mark on the old couple. Two years before they had accomplished their pilgrimage, and now spent their days quietly, content to have achieved the status of *Hajji* and *Hajja*, conferred respectively upon men and women returned from Mecca.

Fourteen years passed before my next visit to the oasis. I arrived to find the village streets paved, electricity available, and several of the earthen-walled houses topped by TV antennas. The old couple had died. Their simple gravestones, bearing no epitaphs, were already lightly covered with drifting sand. Soon they would vanish from view altogether. Unglazed earthen jars held water for the deceased. Burned by the sun and eroded by drifting sand, the jars were themselves crumbling into sand.

At the Sahara's southern fringe, in a region known as the Sahel, desert gives way to savanna. The first time I ever set foot in the Sahel, after crossing the desert no-man's-land, was in April 1975. The heat was terrible, nearly 50°C, and a sandstorm had raged for days, limiting visibility to almost nothing. If the northern desert, with its beautiful sand hills, is characterized by a scorched, vacant stillness, the Sahel, swept by hot windy blasts, is an inferno.

Inhabiting this wilderness, in astonishing numbers, are herds of oxen. You often see them bounding over the scorched, withered grass. Unlike cattle taking their ease in a pasture, these beasts, large and lean, are the survivors of an unremitting struggle for existence. Their feral appearance is the natural result.

Shepherds drove the oxen to a well. Other animals watered there too. Camels, goats and other livestock jostled each other as a crowd of men busied themselves scooping up water. So much life depended on this one well.

The rope, pulled by camels and donkeys, was surprisingly long, extending nearly 100 m from the edge of the well. So the well was 330 ft (100 m) deep.

Year after year, with the Sahel growing drier and drier, the people dug deeper and deeper, until at last the well reached its present precipitous depth.

On the edge of the well is a concrete water tank. The oxen fix their starved gaze on the water in it. The shepherd with a stick lightly taps the lead ox on the horn, at which signal the herd swarms to the water. Knocking horns, they drink greedily. When the herd has drunk its fill, it is led away immediately and the one waiting behind it drinks in turn. The well bucket, attached to a wooden pulley whose creaking sounds like anguished screaming, is pulled incessantly in all directions. Every sudden gust of wind raises blinding clouds of sand and dust that seem to shut out everything in the world – everything except the heart-rending wail of the pulley.

Ten years later, with Africa in the throes of a major drought, a friend of mine passed through that vicinity and found an eerie stillness prevailing. Not a trace of life was to be seen, he said; not so much as a footprint; drifting sand covered everything. Six years after that I myself returned, and the beasts were back, thronging as thickly as before. The well was exactly as it had been, the pulley screeching no less pathetically. The underground water network had come back to life.

As before, hot wind and sand dominated the environment. In this part of the world, life is water, and water, when it exists at all, is 330 feet (100 m) underground. Man and beast alike are reduced to living water bags passing in and out of the fragile water cycle.

"Do ants crawling on the ground even know humans exist?. . ."

That's the kind of thought the Sahara inspires. In May 1975 my wife and I traveled south through the desert in a Land Rover we brought over from Europe. In Niger we made a U-turn, crossing the eastern Tenere Desert into Algeria. Unlike other trans-Sahara routes, this one bore hardly any traffic. Part of the adventure was, ours being the only car on the road, that we could not take safety for granted.

The white-hot horizon seemed to waver in the bloated sun as we forged ahead, following as best we could the countless wheel ruts that were all we had by which to orient ourselves. It took courage at first. Later we noticed marker poles lining the track at regular intervals. At least, we thought with relief, there was no longer any danger of losing the road.

With the setting sun comes the characteristic desert cold, and the temperature dips sharply. Stopping before it got dark, we spread our mattresses on the sand and lay down, basking in the gentleness of evening, recovering our nervous equilibrium after the heat and tension of the day. The sun sank lower and lower. Darkness thickened by the minute. In the clear night sky the stars began to twinkle. Not a sign of life anywhere; not a sound; nothing but the movement of the stars to mark the flow of time.

Sometimes, in times and places like this, I'd catch myself thinking how strange it all was. Might there be another world, its reality unfolding separately from ours but standing in the same physical relationship to us as, say, one side of a piece of paper to the other? Ants, for example, go about their business in highly organized societies without the faintest awareness of the existence of human beings. That being the case, it was not so very disconcerting to speculate on the existence of a still higher race of beings, looking down on us lying on our mattresses in the Tenere Desert in much the same way we might look down on a squirming swarm of ants.

I have spent, cumulatively, nearly two years traveling the Sahara. One day in particular stands out in my mind: June 28, 1975. On that day I witnessed the slaughter of a camel.

It happened in the Fezzan, a sandy expanse in the south of Libya. The day before we had attached ourselves to a camel caravan heading north from neighboring Chad. Ten men were attending 264 camels being transported for their meat. The terrain was totally flat, and there was nothing but sand as far as the eye could see. As for me, I was tagging along in a Land Rover, photographing the scene from different angles.

By day, the caravan drivers judged direction by the shadows; by night, they followed the North Star. During the three hours that the sun was directly overhead and cast no shadows, the party rested. Otherwise they proceeded without pausing, continuing on right through the night. To linger in this wilderness of sand is taboo. Speed is of the essence. A caravan of 264 camels is a vast herd; its ranks seem endless; and yet once, having let them get some distance ahead of me, I looked up to find them reduced to mere specks against the vast desert landscape, their countless footprints imprinted on the sand the only evidence that they were not a mirage.

Suddenly one camel fell behind. It was just past 10:00 in the morning. The caravan stopped for a rest.

The men ate their simple lunch, then set about slaughtering the weakened camel. The desert is a heartless environment. Taking pity on one poor beast is out of the question. Binding the animal's feet and trunk so that it couldn't move, the men pinned it down and thrust a knife into the base of its neck.

In an instant the white stand was blood-red; the stench of blood filled the dry air. Through a torrent of blood I saw the animal's slashed neck tendon. When it had breathed its last the men slit its belly and began dismembering it. This slaughter of a beast bigger than a horse in the midst of a vast desert expanse was an astonishing sight. It was unnerving. Not to the other camels, though. They stood no more than 100 feet (30 m) away looking on apparently unmoved. Working quickly, the men cut away the choice meat and, leaving the rest of the carcass to rot, set the herd in motion and resumed their journey.

Before setting out, the men ceremoniously purified their blood-caked hands and faces with sand and, facing Mecca, bowing deeply and repeatedly, prayed intently. The shadows lengthened in the waning afternoon. The northward trek proceeded uneventfully. The camels' hooves made a dry sound against the sand. The procession seemed a mirage against the clear blue sky. And yet I could not forget that against this backdrop, a backdrop like a scroll depicting the Japanese song "Tsuki no Sabaku" – "The Moonlit Desert" – there had occurred that slaughter so appalling to a stranger.

26-27 Camel-drivers pray in the direction of Mecca before their caravan sets out. They navigate using the sun by day and the stars at night.

28-29 The Algerian-Niger frontier today
is a desperately arid region – and yet
surviving wall paintings thousands of
years old depict flourishing vegetation.

30-31 A basalt pinnacle in the Ahaggar
Mountains of southern Algeria – vestige
of volcanic activity some 2 million years
ago.

32-33 Sand dunes bathed in the golden
light of the evening sun. Saharan sand,
generally pale brown, can change color
from minute to minute depending on
the position of the sun.

34-35 A boy hurries home along a pass through sand dunes glowing in the sunset. In western Algeria giant sand dunes extend to the very edges of the oases.

36-37 A nomad woman searches for camel dung to use as fuel.

38-39 A Tuareg family in torrid northern Niger, living in a traditional tent-dwelling made from tanned livestock hides sewn together.

40-41 Tuareg nomads cope with drought as best they can. Desertification, first noticeable in the 1970s, continues apace.

42-43 The chief of a Moorish tribe of the western Sahara, a region currently ruled by Morocco.

44-45 A young Tuareg tribesman. Tuareg tradition has it that a man who bares his face is unprincipled and not to be trusted.

46-47 Tuareg guide and driver take
their ease in a campground. Even the
stillest nights can be assailed without
warning by raging sandstorms.

49 Tuareg nomads lead their caravan camels through clouds of dust to a watering place.

50-51 The little river that seems to flow in the wake of a caravan crossing the scorching sands of southern Libya is, of course, a mirage.

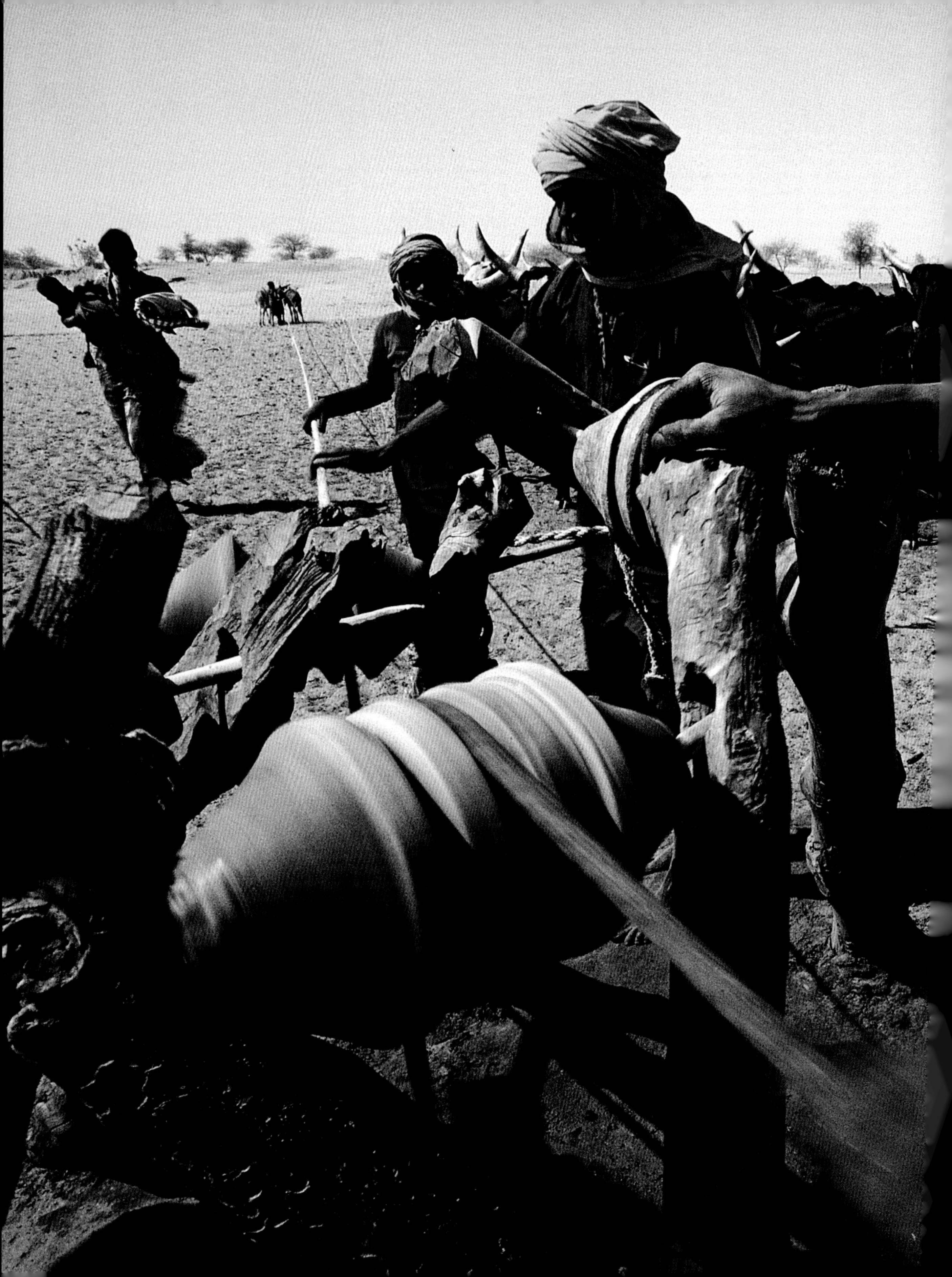

52-53 Tuareg nomads and their goats rest as best they can in the chill winter wind blowing through the Ahaggar Mountains.

54-55 A succession of droughts in the Sahel, the semi-desert southern fringe of the Sahara, has made it necessary to extend wells to a depth of 100 meters. The well bucket is drawn up by livestock.

56-57 Livestock crowding round a well in the Sahel. The well is equipped with an electric pump. Nomads must be alert to make sure their herds don't get mixed up.

Marocco
High Atlas

58-59 In a valley 2200 meters high in the
High Atlas Mountains is the village of
Imilchil. Separated from Sahara and
Mediterranean climates by steep cliffs,
each valley has managed to preserve its
own unique traditional culture.

60-61 A young woman of Imilchil minds her grazing sheep. The pattern on her cape symbolizes the clan to which she belongs.

62-63 Early winter in the Atlas Mountains. A family returns from the regular village market.

64-65 Nomads descending the mountain, their baggage carried down the steep slopes by horses and mules.

66-67 A man wearing a jellabah, a Moroccan
tribal garment. It is standard dress in the Atlas
Mountains, where winter cold is extreme.

68 A young Berber arriving at a Mousem
(Festival of the Saints).

69 A young boy studying the Quran at a
madrassa, an Islamic religious school.

71 Young Berber girls in a mountain valley village. Each valley has its own characteristic clothing.

72-73 A nomad family living 8910 ft (2700 m)
up in the mountains. Compared to the desert,
the High Atlas is blessed with abundant
pasture.

74-75 A young mother nurses her child in the kitchen of her home. Unlike their Arab counterparts, Berber women don't cover their faces, and have no sense of taboo about being photographed.

76-77 An old woman and her granddaughter relax in their tent. In the eastern High Atlas Mountains stretch vast pasture lands on which Berber nomads graze great herds of sheep.

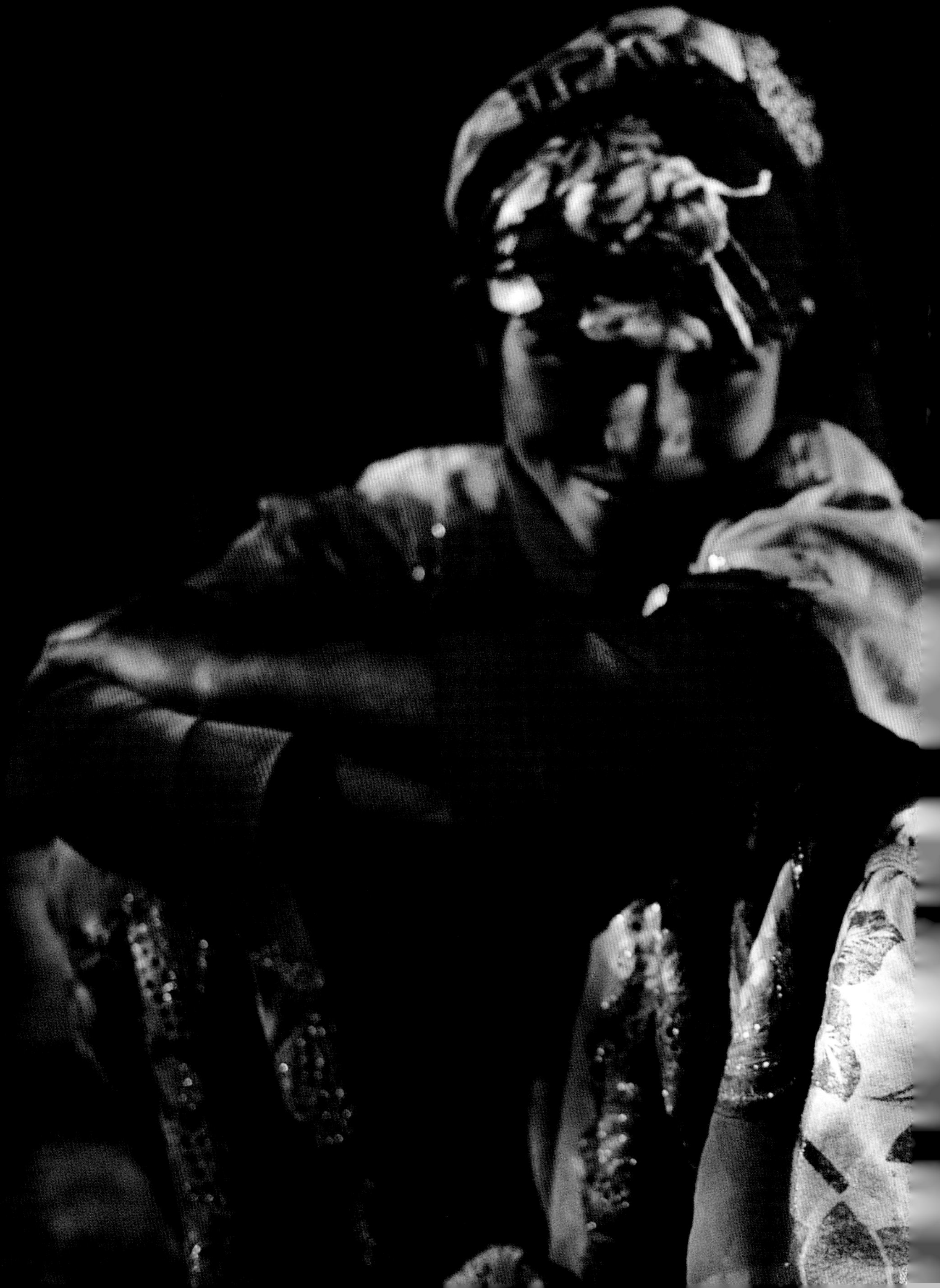

79 A High Atlas Berber farm wife stands in her smoky kitchen,
her form illuminated by sunlight streaming in through the window.

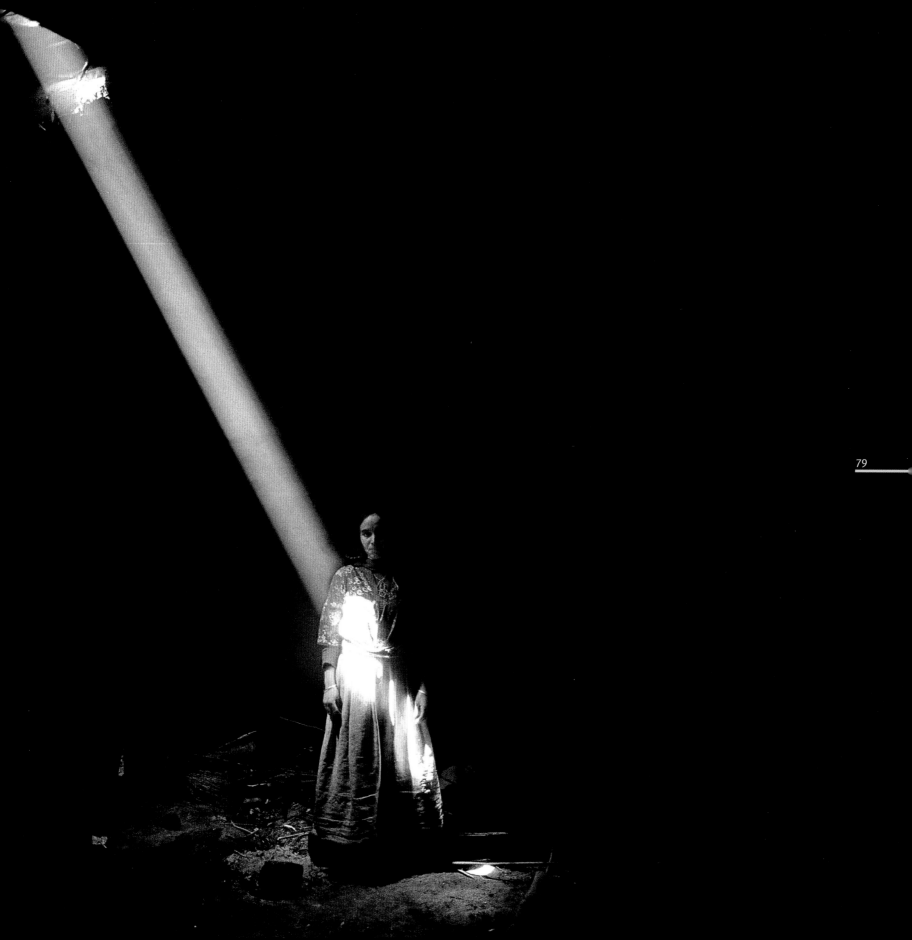

80 and 80-81 The biggest sheep market in the High
Atlas Mountains, held in conjunction with the Imilchil
Mousem (Festival of the Saints), which the Berbers
of the region celebrate in September.

82-83 People celebrating Mousem in the holy city of Boujad, 124 miles (200 km) south of Rabat. The descendants of saints enshrined in mausolea set up a sprawling tent village, where they gather over several days to promote friendship.

84-85 An elderly participant in the
Boujad Mousem. Even those
descendants working in Europe return
home once a year for Mousem.

The medinas

Old urban quarters trapped in the Middle Ages

86-87 The medina (old quarter) of Fez.
Fez is the birthplace of Moroccan Islamic
culture. Surrounded by walls, it spreads
out on all sides from the Karaouiyne
Mosque, North Africa's oldest, at its center.

88-89 An old person shuffles through the hilly streets of the old quarter of Chechaouene, a city nestled in the mountains of northern Morocco. Its white walls are strikingly beautiful.

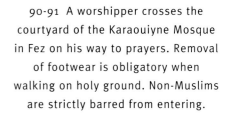

90-91 A worshipper crosses the courtyard of the Karaouiyne Mosque in Fez on his way to prayers. Removal of footwear is obligatory when walking on holy ground. Non-Muslims are strictly barred from entering.

92-93 People waiting for an early-morning inter-city bus in the old quarter of Rabat.

94-95 Arab women
dressed in black.
Arab society in eastern
Morocco is relatively
strict.

97 A woman sells homemade bread at dusk on a street corner of the old quarter of Marrakech.

98-99 One winter morning in the Atlas Mountain village of Imilchil, a child basks in the sun.

100-101 This Fez dye works specializes
in animal hides. The vivid colors are in
stark contrast to the overwhelming
stench. The roadside is littered with
freshly severed cow and sheep heads.

Brides
of the High Atlas

103 A bride all decked out in her finery. Every year, in September, when tens of thousands of people gather in Imilchil for Mousem, young people celebrate their engagement to marry with elaborate ceremonies.

104 and 104-105 The Berber tribe Ait Yazza, which
lives in the vicinity of Imilchil, holds its mass
engagement ceremony for young girls (the ceremony
is called *tamaghara* in the Berber language) apart
from the Mousem engagement ceremonies.

106-107 The *tamaghara*, arranged by
the parents of young people of
marriageable age, takes place every
four or five years. Strangely enough,
almost all couples who meet here
divorce within a year of marriage.
Some divorce after only a week.
Afterwards, the men and women
associate freely with one another,
marrying and divorcing repeatedly,
until at last they settle down and start
stable families. Here is a rare and
peculiar example of a custom wholly at
odds with the general Islamic
strictness concerning sexual relations.

108 and 108-109 All the girls of the family, down to the age of 12, adorn themselves as brides, first undergoing a medical examination by the village health officer in order to obtain written proof of virginity.

110-111 Accompanied by songs and the beating of drums, brides mounted on mules proceed to the marriage ceremony as grooms assembled on a rooftop look down on the scene. Mass weddings of young maidens are an Ait Yazza custom, a rite of passage into adulthood.

THE ROOF OF THE WORLD

TIBET

BUDDHISM'S
HIGH COUNTRY

TIBET

BUDDHISM'S HIGH COUNTRY

$\bullet\!\!\!\!\rightarrow$

AT THE HEART OF THE EURASIAN LANDMASS, BORDERED BY THE HIMALAYA, KUNLUN, KARAKORAM AND MIN MOUN-TAIN RANGES, LIES THE VAST TIBETAN PLATEAU.

Tibetans, devout Buddhists, liken the mountains to lotus flowers; Tibet itself, they say, is a pure land blessed by Avalokiteshvara, the god of mercy. Until recently, Tibet, a natu-ral fortress thanks to its mountainous land-scape and long isolated from the outside world, was a peaceful Buddhist country.

With its limpid air, countless lakes, snow-covered mountains and grassy steppes, the plateau presents a spectacle of stunning beau-ty – deceptive beauty, in a sense, for it adorns the harshest living environment imaginable. Some agriculture is possible along the valleys; otherwise, the Tibetan plateau, 13,200 ft (4000 m) above sea level, is a cold, boundless expanse where not even trees can grow. It is a nomad's world, this "fourth polar region." The three summer months yield their meager quantity of pasturage; during the rest of the year, the al-most perpetually frozen ground yields nothing. Ages ago humans tamed the wild yak, and now depend on it, as a parasite depends on its host, for clothing, food and shelter.

With no trees to cut down, yak dung is the only available fuel. In winter, when tempera-tures hover around 30ºC below zero, life would be bleak indeed without the stove burning all day long in the center of the yak-hair tent, and the comfort of hot butter-tea. With pasturage so scarce, the beasts produce almost no milk at all during the winter. Every morning, after putting the yaks out to graze, the nomads gather the dung that fell overnight, the women tossing it into baskets strapped to their backs. Watching them, I had a vivid sense of what an irreplaceable fuel pro-ducer the yak is. Yak dung burns a long time. It is just the fuel Tibet needs.

And yak-hair tents, waterproof and resist-ant to the strong winds, are the perfect shelter. The circulation inside is good. Being black, they absorb heat, so that during the day at least the interior is quite warm.

112 Monks en route to their devotions through the falling snow.

115 The Sutlej River flows down from the Mt. Kailas range through a savage landscape.

The nomads' diet consists mostly of dairy products, supplemented by meat from livestock they slaughter themselves. The bulk of their calorie intake comes from the tens of cups of butter tea they drink daily. Other foods include processed barley preparation called tsampa, cha-bagchung brick tea, and salt from the salty lakes of the Chang Tang plateau.

In the highlands, the frozen earth is covered by a one-foot (30-cm) cushion of topsoil, formed over hundreds of years in the humus layer, with its admixture of tangled grass roots. The cushion, once lost, would be irrecoverable – the highland would turn to desert in no time. The grass that grows in this fragile topsoil is the first link in the food chain. It nourishes the livestock. Tibetans have traditionally regarded land development as taboo – perhaps because of the Buddhist view of life sustained by their unique environment. It's a view of life permeated by the notion of transmigration, nowhere seen more vividly than in the Tibetan custom of sky burial.

A corpse, once the priests have said the requisite prayers over the deceased and sent the soul on its way, is regarded as no more dignified than a sloughed-off skin, fit food for vultures. Accordingly it is chopped up and fed to them, the human body continuing after death to be part of the local ecosystem. There is no alternative in any case, firewood being lacking for cremation and the frozen ground, retarding decomposition, making burial impossible.

Sky burial ceremonies are strictly off-limits to any outsider, let alone a foreigner, but with luck, I managed to be present at one. It happened one morning, just after I'd left a small town in eastern Tibet. Along the road were numerous prayer flags called *tharchok* – markers, in that part of the country, of sacred space. A wisp of smoke rose. What was going on? I asked my guide. Probably, he said, birds were being summoned for a sky burial. Was it possible? Speechless, I gazed at the rising smoke. Outside the sacred ground three men with two horses were resting. They had brought the body here. The deceased, they said, was an eleven-year-old girl who had died from a ruptured liver after being thrown from a horse. Even as we listened, some thirty vultures arrived, flying low over a hut within the ceremonial enclosure.

The dismemberment of the corpse began. Camera in hand, I went behind the *tharchok* some 165 ft (50 m) away. What would they do when they saw me? But the men paid no attention to me. A priest in an apron laid the corpse on a stone in front of the hut, and began cutting away. Now standing, now squatting, he wielded hatchet and knives with practiced hands. Every time he rose to his feet I saw fresh bloodstains on his apron.

A watchman crouched in a corner of the hut, making sure the birds didn't attack prematurely. The priest rested frequently in his work; sometimes he and the watchman would chat together, laughing. You'd think it was a sheep being dismembered on that fine summer day, so free and easy was everyone. The priest would work for a time and then,

117　A stupa, weathered by the wind, in Toling, western Tibet.

A Toling temple stupa, bathed in afternoon sunlight. Toling, the center of Western Tibetan Buddhism around the 11th century, is home to more than 100 stupas, some of them fallen into ruin as a result of wind erosion.

holding aloft a severed arm or some other part, pause briefly, and resume his banter with the watchman.

Finally, after about twenty minutes' work, the priest tossed two chunks of flesh in the direction of the hovering birds. That was the signal they had been waiting for. They swarmed to their dinner table. The feast began. It was over in a twinkling. Having eaten their fill, the birds flew off into the cloudy late-afternoon sky. So this was sky burial, the dead presented as an offering to the living. To Tibetans this is natural and right. To me, though, it was a shattering spectacle. Heading back to the car after finishing my photography, it was all I could do to stay on my feet, so shaken was I.

120-121 Ruins of the Guge
Kingdom are visible on
Tsaparang Hill (center). The
Guge Kingdom throve for 600
years, but in 1630 was
overthrown by Ladakh.

122-123 Panoramic view from
the Guge Kingdom ruins of the
Tsaparang moonscape. Bathed
in the light of the setting sun,
the silent scene is suggestive
of the end of the world. The
contours we see today are the
results of erosion on mud that
accumulated long ago at the
bottom of the lake.

124-125 Nuns proceed round the giant boulders towering over holy Lake Namtso, north of Lhasa. The two boulders are believed to be the lake's protector gods.

126-127 On the festival known as Labab Duchen, pilgrims circumnavigate a hill on which stands a stupa. Labab Duchen is celebrated on the 15th day of the 9th month of the Tibetan calendar. On this day, Gautama Buddha descends from heaven to answer the supplications of mothers.

128-129 Two nomad worshippers at
Labab Duchen awake from a night's
sleep in the open. The nighttime
temperature in mid-November here
at 15,510 ft (4700 m) above sea level
falls to -10°C.

Winter

GRAZING LAND

130-131 Around October, the nomads come
down from their summer grazing grounds high
in the mountains to the foothills. Here, with
houses and left-over pasturage to help them
through the harsh weather, they pass the winter.

132-133 A nomad girl has applied *tocha* to her face. *Tocha* is a cosmetic made from either concentrated buttermilk or roots. It protects the skin from ultraviolet rays and dryness.

134

134-135 A nomad girl of Western Tibet.
The region, 16,500 ft (5000 m) above
sea level, is snowed in even in June.

136-137 A nomad child travels comfortably in a basket mounted on a yak's back. Yaks used to carry people have their horns cut off for safety.

138-139 This photo was taken in
November. During the worst of the
winter, drinking water is obtained by
cutting into ice 12 inches (30 cm) thick.

140 and 140-141 Salt caravaneers take a break. Dried-out salt lakes abound throughout the Tibetan highlands, which in ancient times were sea beds. The salt extracted from the dried lakes is transported and sold as far away as Nepal.

142 and 143 The life cycle in these extreme altitudes begins with the scant pasturage. Humans could hardly survive without their livestock, depending on them for milk, meat, and the only available fuel – animal dung.

144 and 144-145 Home to the nomads is a black yak-
hair tent. The tents hold firm against the strongest
wind, absorb heat so that it's quite warm inside during
the day, and afford excellent circulation.

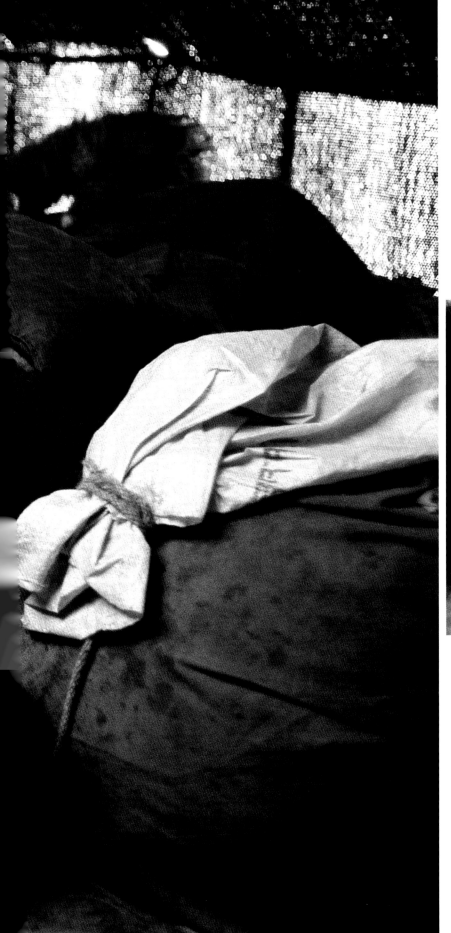

146-147 and 147 Though in mid-winter it's -20°C
outside, the nomads sleep naked under their
blankets. Their warm breath mingling with the cold
air causes the blankets to become covered with frost.

148 and 149 In the cold of the Tibetan highlands, bathing is a rarity. A certain amount of dirt provides a healthy protection for the skin against the extreme dryness of the air.

150-151 The brand new classroom portraits of the
heroes of the revolution are in sharp contrast to the
unwashed children. The learning environment in primary
schools in rural Tibet is very bad, which perhaps
explains the chronically low attendance.

MOUNT KAILAS

MOUNTAIN OF THE GODS, AXIS OF THE UNIVERSE

K AILAS, THE MOUNTAIN OF THE GODS, SOARS PRECIPITOUSLY OVER THE WESTERN TIBETAN WILDERNESS.

I first saw it in a 1984 television documentary. It was breathtaking. The accounts I'd heard of it hardly did it justice. But it was less the mountain itself that kept my eyes glued to the screen than the pilgrims making their way to it with such single-minded devotion. Among them was a one-legged Hindu. Leaning on a cane, he had walked from Calcutta, had been on the road twenty years; one step at a time he had hobbled up the Himalayas; now he was at a height of 16,500-ft (5000 m). Nor was his the only extraordinary feat. There were pilgrims who had proceeded at a devotional crawl all the way from eastern Tibet. They too had been traveling for twenty years.

How strange, the survival of all this amid the relentless, irresistible standardization of modern times – people so intent on their souls' afterlife that without a second thought they commit their entire lives to the pilgrimage to Mt. Kailas. The one-legged Hindu, the Tibetan pilgrims advancing on their bellies at their tortuous snail's pace – these were not priestly ascetics but simple, ordinary people. What magnetic force does Mt. Kailas exert on them? Whatever it was, this was a

mountain I had to see with my own eyes. The trouble was, one needed special permission back then to travel to Mt. Kailas. Politically and physically, the western Tibetan interior was as inaccessible a place as any on earth.

My chance came in May 1990. A friend of mine, a TV director, had been filming in the Himalayas and was on his way to Mt. Kailas. By dint of a good deal of persuasion, I managed to get myself included in the expedition. Its purpose was to film the Saga Dawa, the festival of the fifteenth day of the fourth month of the Tibetan calendar, commemorating the Buddha's birthday, the day of his death and the day he attained enlightenment. That year the Saga Dawa fell on June 8 of the Western calendar. By the Chinese calendar it was the Year of the Horse. To undertake a pilgrimage to Mt. Kailas during Saga Dawa in the Year of the Horse, which comes around once every twelve years, is to acquire the highest possible merit.

The plan was to meet up with the four-man TV crew in the Nepalese capital of Kathmandu, then proceed to the border town of Zangmu, where our Tibetan staff would be waiting to help us with the crossing. Naturally there was trouble. The Tibetan interpreter must have said something that rubbed the Chinese bor-

153 The northern face of Mt. Kailas, bathed in the light of the morning sun. Tibetans call Kailas "Khang Rinpoche" – Precious Jewel of Snow.

154 Innumerable prayer flags mark a holy spot where a pilgrim offers up prayers. Prayer flags
like these are frequent sights in eastern Tibet.

157 A pilgrim covered with dust performing a devotional crawl.

der guard the wrong way; the guard abruptly shut the office and decamped, leaving us stuck in Zangmu. It was two days before we got underway. To make up for lost time we skipped the rests we'd planned and drove without pausing, straight through the 16,665 ft (5050 m) pass into the Plateau of Tibet. It was insane, of course – not so much for my four companions, who had already acclimatized themselves to the high altitude in Nepal, as for me, who had not.

Just as the chest pains that had been bothering me in the pass began to ease, my head started to ache and I felt feverish. We drove on until dusk, then we set up our tent in a windswept open field. The wind was not the gentle monsoon breeze of the day before, but a cold winter blast. For supper I tried slurping some instant ramen noodles, but was too wretchedly nauseous to get anything down. I spent the whole night throwing up. Lovely, I thought. There's only one cure for altitude sickness: returning to the lowlands. Ahead of us the high country stretched on and on, altitude nearly 16,500 ft (5000 m), as far as the eye could see. Our little tent rattled in the stiff wind. Dawn came, and I hadn't slept a wink. Off to the east, near Chomolungma, the top of Cho Oyu (27,063 ft; 8201 m) was tinted deep red; I watched it slowly whiten, too nauseous to reach for my camera.

We folded up our tent and hit the road.

The sharp morning light cast long vivid shadows on the bare mountain slopes. I'd often seen shadows like this in the desert, but here in the thin air the light was sword-point sharp, and the effect that much more dramatic. Wild rabbits startled by our vehicle's invasion of their moonscape habitat darted madly about, their panicked flight leaving us far behind. They breed like locusts, and

Tibetans, devout Buddhists who shrink from killing of any kind, don't interfere with them. The image of those panicked rabbits stayed with me long after they had vanished. My headache and nausea showed no sign of abating. Small swellings broke out on my hands and face. This was the price I was paying for not having properly acclimatized myself. The effects lasted throughout the trip. When it was over I found I'd lost almost 16 lbs (7 kg).

Three days' driving brought us to western Tibet's Chang Tang plateau, where the mean altitude is 16,170 ft (4900 m). Beyond the reach of monsoon rains, this highland region is all but bare even of grass, let alone trees. In a gray valley sits a lake so blue it is almost eerie. The sky was clear but for a single oddly shaped cloud – it made me think of the curious round clouds you sometimes see in Tibetan religious paintings. Snow was falling steadily from it.

Once, large flakes of snow began to fall from a clear sky, blurring everything around us. Was the lack of oxygen playing tricks with my eyes? Everything I saw seemed to feed the impression that I was hallucinating.

On the evening of the seventh day after leaving Zangmu we saw Mt. Kailas. It was the driver who pointed it out. To me at first sight it seemed insignificant, hardly worthy of notice. Only as we drew near did its aloof, pyramid-shaped grandeur reveal itself.

Here we were at last. A strange mountain. Glowing in the setting sun were intersecting cracks running now vertically, now horizontally along its southern face. They were *manji*, said someone – Indian swastikas, symbols of good fortune. So they were. What an oddly shaped mountain, quite unlike any other. Khang Rinpoche, the Tibetans call it – Jewel of Snows. Contemplating it, I seemed to grasp something of the religious ecstasy that seizes pilgrims who gaze up at it at the end of a long, arduous, prayerful pilgrimage.

"Sins are washed clean at the sight of the Himalayas. This is because Mount Kailas and Lake Manasarowar are there," says the ancient proverb.

In the foothills of Mt. Kailas is Dharchen, which pilgrims use as a base. We arrived to find nearly five hundred tents accommodating some five thousand pilgrims. In the middle of the night I was awakened by thudding footsteps outside our tent. The pilgrims were on the move, bound for a circular mountain road 32 miles (52 km) in circumference. The Tibetans walk it clockwise, returning to camp exhausted more than ten hours later. Then they rest two or three days, and do it again, and again, trekking round and round Mt. Kailas. By dint of repeated penance they hope to wash away their sins in order to be reborn as human beings, so that they may continue to accumulate merit toward the ultimate goal of freedom from worldly attachment.

Suffering from altitude sickness, gasping for breath, we could hardly hope to keep up with them. With eight hired porters, it took us four days to complete one lap. Buddhist pilgrimages are always, not only at Mt. Kailas, clockwise. Bon pilgrims (Bon is a shamanistic Tibetan religion pre-dating Buddhism), on the other hand, proceed counter-clockwise.

The road sloped gently enough at first, but every uphill grade was enough to wind me. Early in the morning of the second day I was being overtaken by pilgrims just setting out. They had left Dharchen before dawn and planned to be back the same evening. They traveled light for speed – emptyhanded except for some wheat flour.

They walked in silence. Here and there were men and women, their faces begrimed with dust, proceeding at a ritualized crawl. Among them, I was surprised to notice, were quite a few young girls.

On the early afternoon of the third day we approached Dolma La Pass, 20,400 ft (5636 m) above sea level. This would be the most difficult part. Slipping in the sherbet-like snow, on the brink of total exhaustion and giddy besides, I climbed, my breath coming in short gasps. Controlling my breathing as best I could, I advanced no more than twenty meters at a time. A young mother, baby strapped to her back, passed me with a look that seemed to say, "What on earth is wrong with him?" Are Tibetan bodies built differently, or what?

At last we were in the pass. Scattered about the exposed bedrock were giant boulders, as big as houses. Prayer flags and banners were everywhere. Stones with passages from the sutras carved on them were piled one on another. The flags fluttered in the wind – a sign that the prayers of the pilgrims were ascending to the gods in heaven.

One after another the pilgrims, shouting "Victory to the gods!", tossed bundles of colored paper prayer charms into the air. The charms fluttered and flapped in the wind, their dancing flight toward Mt. Kailas – a beautiful sight. Offering brief prayers, their faces radiant, the pilgrims set off, striding rapidly along the descending path.

Mt. Kailas, axis of the universe according to popular belief, draws an endless stream of pilgrims performing life-renewing, life-cleansing religious observances. It was my good fortune, climax to an arduous journey, to be able to see some of what goes on there with my own eyes.

158-159 Pilgrims circumnavigating Mt. Kailas. Buddhist pilgrims invariably proceed clockwise around holy sites. Bon pilgrims, however, walk counter-clockwise. One circuit is 32 miles (52 km) along a mountain road – a trek the robust Tibetans accomplish in one day.

160-161 Pilgrims advancing at a devotional crawl around Mt. Kailas. The crawl proceeds regardless of the terrain, and some of it – frozen earth, small rivers, snowy ravines – is very rough indeed.

162 and 163 To crawl round Mt. Kailas through a mountain pass 32 miles (52 km) long at an altitude of 18,600 ft (5636 m) takes about two weeks. This ardent pilgrim is on his way again after a short rest at the foothills.

164-165 This pilgrim on her way to a stupa
counts on her Buddhist prayer beads the
number of devotional crawls she has performed.

LHASA

PURE LAND OF THE BUTTER LAMPS

ONE EVENING IN LHASA, RETURNING EXHAUSTED TO MY HOTEL AFTER HAVING SPENT THE ENTIRE DAY PHOTOGRAPHING TEMPLES, I BLEW MY NOSE AND FOUND MY HANDKERCHIEF STAINED BLACK. WHAT WAS THIS? WHAT IN THE PURE, CLEAR HIGHLAND AIR COULD ACCOUNT FOR SUCH FILTH?

The culprits, it turned out, were butter-fueled votive lamps. These burn in profusion in Tibetan temples everywhere, in the spacious halls in front of the statues of Buddha and Rama. The largest of them are set in giant pan-like stands three feet (1 m) in diameter, the pans filled with butter. In each pan, several wicks of twisted cotton burn all day long. On festival days hundreds of burning lamps set in small bowls brighten the hall, filling it with soot and the smell of fat.

Throngs of pilgrims stream through the halls, reverently laying butter they have brought with them on the lamp stands as they pray. Pools of spilled butter form on the floor; it squelches unpleasantly under your feet and sticks to the soles of your shoes. The thick curtain partitions in the halls are stained and greasy with butter. All this is as different as can be from old temples in Japan, whose incense, Zen gardens, shoji paper screens and pleasantly cool wooden corridors may form a some-

what artificial Buddhist atmosphere but are clean and bracing all the same.

The giant Buddha statues enshrined in those Tibetan temple halls smelling of fat glitter with gilding. Most of them are new, built in the 1980s to replace those destroyed in the Cultural Revolution. The vermilion lips and glaring eyes, bursting with vigor, are not in the best of taste. Tarnished statues of Buddha and Rama are regularly retouched with layers of gold paint. It is not aesthetics, however, that draws the believers, some of whom crawl on the floor through the spilt butter, making a sloshing sound as they go. Approaching the principal image, they lay bare their hearts and chant mantras before resuming their holy crawl.

Such fervor is overpowering, almost frightening. The other face of the Tibetan character, though, is the gentleness fostered by Buddhist philosophy. Deeply rooted in that character is belief in the laws of karma. All living things are eternally reincarnated, one's present incarnation the natural consequence of the course of one's previous life. Every insect, every bird, is potentially a reincarnated member of one's own family.

To people who regard all living things as equal members of a single body of life, the notion of killing flies, mosquitoes, even harmful organisms, is

167 Pilgrims paying their respects at Lhasa's Jokhang Temple. Jokhang is the head temple of Tibetan Buddhism.

unthinkable. Fortunately Tibet's dry highland climate is inhospitable to harmful insects. In removing fleas from his head, a Tibetan will take great pains not to crush them, pulling out two or three hairs and setting the bugs free in them.

When I asked Tibetan refugees in torrid India how they coped with their far greater mosquito problem, they said they burned insect-repellent incense – and made a point of leaving a window open to allow the bugs to escape.

Some devout individuals go to abbatoirs to purchase livestock about to be slaughtered, then raise the beasts to the end of their natural lives. Or a family nursing a sick relative might rescue an animal from the slaughterers in the belief that the merit thus acquired will help cure the sufferer. The all-embracing kind-heart-edness of Tibetans leaves a deep impression on foreign visitors. In 1946 the Austrian mountain-eer Heinrich Harrer arrived in Lhasa, and was astonished to observe a construction site thrown into turmoil by the appearance of an insect. Work ground to a halt as everyone's attention focused on rescuing the bug. Harrer described the scene movingly in *Seven Years in Tibet*.

168-169 Pilgrims from all over Tibet
throng Jokhang Temple – especially
in autumn, when the harvest is over.

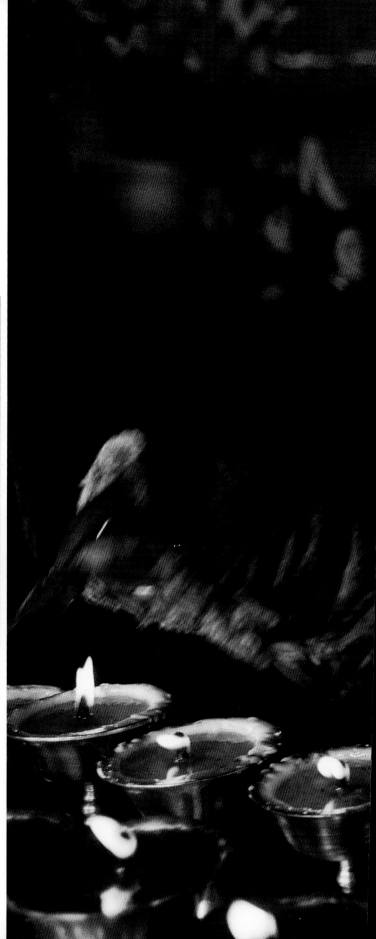

170 and 170-171 Tibetan pilgrims in their richly distinct
regional garb, rich and poor alike, converge on Jokhang
Temple, many of them pouring into votive lamps butter they
have brought with them especially for the purpose.

172-173 A pilgrim unfurls his *khata*, a ceremonial scarf. When meeting a high priest, or when praying at any holy place, pilgrims offer up their *khatas*.

174-175 After a hard morning's devotions, a young monk rests wrapped in the priestly garment that had earlier been worn by a senior priest.

176-177 Priests quenching their thirst with milk
tea. In the harsh environment of western Tibet
most people drink high-calorie butter tea, but
eastern Tibetans prefer milk tea.

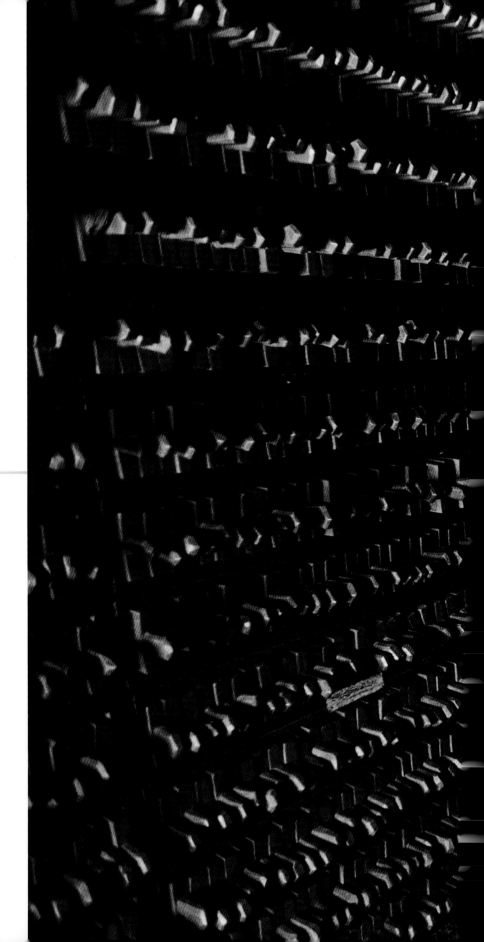

178-179 In Derge Parkhang in eastern Tibet are
stored some 300,000 wood-carved printing boards.
There were formerly three presses in Tibet for
printing *sutras*, but the other two were destroyed in
the Cultural Revolution, and today Derge Parkhang
alone remains.

180-181 The hands of a nun hold the loose leaves of a scripture-book, known in Tibetan as *pecha*. The nun's hands are smeared with butter to protect them against the winter dryness.

MONLAM CHENMO

THE GREAT PRAYER FESTIVAL

O
N THE EXTREME NORTHEASTERN EDGE OF TIBET'S SPHERE OF CULTURAL INFLUENCE IS THE LABRANG TASHIKYIL MONASTERY IN CHINA'S GANSU PROVINCE. IN LATE FEBRUARY 2002 THE MONASTERY WAS FILLED TO BURSTING WITH PILGRIMS COME TO CELEBRATE THE HUGE PRAYER MEETING KNOWN AS MONLAM.

Monlam begins on the fourth day of the Tibetan New Year and ends with a rousing climax spanning the 13th, 14th and 15th days. Friction between officials who conceived the notion of staging Monlam as a tourist draw in the holy city of Lhasa and monks opposed to the idea sparked riots in 1989 that led to the imposition of martial law. To this day Monlam is not celebrated in Lhasa. Farther east, however, where Tibetans have a long history of untroubled intercourse with Chinese, Monlam unfolds as it always has, with great pomp and ceremony.

I first visited Labrang Tashikyil in 1989. The first thing that struck me on my second visit thirteen years later was the change in the pilgrims' attire. Earlier, cocooned against the -15°C cold in none-too-clean fur coats called *chubas*, they had approached the shrine looking like hungry ghosts or the angry Buddhist demon Asura. Today – such

are the fruits of economic growth – the nomads are well dressed, and one notes an air of refined elegance in their faces.

Another change: there are now numerous Chinese pilgrims among the worshippers. A Chinese presence in a Tibetan temple would earlier have been unthinkable. But the recent economic development, riddled with contradictions, has been emotionally unsettling to such a degree that people find they need something to believe in.

As religion has spread among ordinary people, popular gadgetry has penetrated religion. Some monks have begun to carry cell phones. Along the road fronting the monastery are public phones that take telephone cards. You can call Japan direct from them – the voice from Tokyo comes through loud and clear; you might almost think you're there; and then suddenly your eye shifts to the street and you see two female pilgrims crawling through the dust as an expression of religious devotion.

Tibet is in the throes of explosive change. In the past, merciless oppression under Chinese communism may have served to unite the Tibetan people, but now there seems no resisting the sweet temptations of prosperity.

183 On the 15th day of Monlam, the Tibetan New Year, monks await the start of prayers under a driving snow.

184-185 Sturdy monks known as Geko, readily identifiable by their distinctive attire, are responsible for managing the Monlam and maintaining public order.

186-187 At the great prayer meeting on the 15th day of the first month it is customary for two priests of superior learning to challenge each other to religious disputation in question-and-answer format. A monk issues a challenge by striking the palm of his hand.

188 and 188-189 A living Buddha and monks. There are
in Tibet more than 1000 living Buddhas, from the Dalai
Lama on down. At large monasteries living Buddhas,
regarded as their predecessors reborn, take charge of
all the institution's affairs.

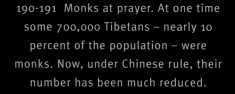

190-191 Monks at prayer. At one time
some 700,000 Tibetans – nearly 10
percent of the population – were
monks. Now, under Chinese rule, their
number has been much reduced.

192-193 Monks carrying a giant applique
thangka. The *thangka* is displayed to the
public once a year at the Labrang
Tashikiyil Monastery Monlam.

194-195 A giant *thangka* unfurled on a
mountain slope. The *thangka*, at first concealed
behind a curtain, is unveiled as excited
believers prostrate themselves in prayer.

196-197 Believers crowd round the seat vacated by
a high-ranking living Buddha who has just presided
over a religious service. It is believed that touching
something that has been touched by a living
Buddha confers good fortune.

198 and 198-199 Wrathful guardian deities adorn the long-handled drums known as *langa*. *Langa* are used during religious festivals and, together with cymbals, during daily religious services.

200-201 The slow-tempo, wordless *cham* masked dance is performed on the 14th day of the first month of the Tibetan calendar in order to subdue evil.

RIVER MOTHER

INDIA

THE NECTAR
OF IMMORTALITY

INDIA

THE NECTAR OF IMMORTALITY

I N LATE APRIL, WITH THE MONSOON STILL A MONTH AWAY, INDIA BRACES FOR ITS HOTTEST SEASON. THE HARVEST IS IN.

The earth, shriveling under the sun's relentless glare, is cracked and dry. Dust swirls in the searing wind. Temperatures rise to 45°C. The streets swarm with pilgrims, a veritable "human flood." Carrying bundles and sacks of provisions on their heads, cradling infants in their arms, they trudge with single-minded resolve from one holy site to another.

In the holy city of Ujjain in central India, Hinduism's greatest bathing festival, the Kumbh Mela, is celebrated every twelve years. The most recent one took place in April 2004. Five days in the month-long festival are especially holy. On these days pilgrims descend on Ujjain from all over the country – 5 to 7 million people, a vast human wave.

A Hindu creation myth has it that gods and demons wound the giant serpent Vaskii around Mt. Mandala and, tugging against one another, churned the Milky Sea, from which emerged the sun, the moon, heaven and earth. Lastly there appeared amrit, the nectar of immortality. As gods and demons fought over it, it spilt, drops of it falling in four places: Allahabad, Haridwar, Nashik, and Ujjain. When the sun, moon and plan-

ets are aligned as they were when the amrit spilt, the amrit's power is reborn, believers say, in the water at the holy sites.

Minute astrological calculation determines the date of the Kumbh Mela. "Kumbh" means "vessel," the vessel containing the nectar; "mela" means "pilgrimage." Each of the four holy sites has a Kumbh Mela every twelve years. A rotation system ensuring there is a Kumbh Mela somewhere in India every three years dates back to ancient times. The 2001 Kumbh Mela in Allahabad, where the Ganges and Yamuna Rivers meet, was a Maha Kumbh, which comes round every 144 years and owes its special significance to the ideal alignment of celestial bodies referred to above. To participate in the ritual bathing of a Maha Kumbh, Hindus believe, is to ensure a future life free from worldly attachment.

Through Ujjain flows the Sipra River, tributary to the Yamuna, which in turn flows into the Ganges. Holy sites in the vicinity of this sacred river – the Mahakala Temple, for example – have a distinguished history dating back to ancient times, and pilgrims form long lines to pay homage to the protector gods enshrined here. The riverbank ghats – concrete steps to facilitate ritual bathing – are similarly thronged with worshippers.

205 A young woman sells lanterns called *arti* on a bank of the Ganges. *Arti* are floated on the
river to send the ancestral spirits on their way.

At the height of the dry season, when the water level sinks and the river is stagnant to the point it hardly seems to be flowing at all, millions bathe in it day after day nonetheless, rendering it filthy from a sanitation point of view. Undaunted, bathers intent on attaining happiness for future lives immerse their bodies in it and take the water into their mouths, the better to wash their sins away. Intoxicated with the supreme bliss of Kumbh Mela, they offer up their prayers.

During the Ujjain Kumbh Mela, tent villages extending more than ten kilometers along both banks of the Sipra River accommodate at any given time some two million pilgrims. Each religious order had its own giant tents, cleverly arranged to constitute a community and filled to bursting with worshippers come to offer reverence to their order's founder. Then there are the *sadhus*, monks in training who also play a leading part in the Kumbh Mela festivities. Kumbh Mela provides the only opportunity for *sadhus* to undergo their initiation ceremony.

Sadhus are symbolic of India's spiritual culture. Severing all family ties, turning their backs on their homes, they live penniless in forests and caves, surviving on the charity of believers and devoting all their time to religious austerities. *Sadhus* are said to constitute 1.3 percent of India's population – 13 million-odd people whose rejection of secular values earns them the approval and respect of the Indian people. Some *sadhus* keep one arm lifted above their heads for years at a time; others bury themselves in the ground, leaving only their heads exposed; others still lie on straw mats studded with needles. By means of austerities and meditation they seek to purify their souls. Some 100,000 *sadhus* take part in a Kumbh Mela. Most conspicuous among them are the few thousand Naga *sadhus* – distinguished from other *sadhus* by their going about stark naked.

Normally they wear loincloths, but at festivals bringing them face to face with the gods they "wear the wind," which is to say they wear nothing. There they were, without a stitch of clothing on them, their entire bodies, lean from their austerities, caked with ash. The first sight of them made me flinch, but when, through my interpreter, I fell into talk with them, I found them surprisingly friendly. Certainly I could photograph them, they said. Within three or four days I was used to them; the sight of their exposed genitalia no longer made me squirm. Many female worshippers came by without a qualm to offer their devotions. Apparently they could do this without arousing any sexual interest on the part of the ascetics.

The climax of the Ujjain Kumbh Mela came early in the morning of April 22. This was when the *sadhus*' bathing reached its peak. It began with a parade of Naga *sadhus*. To accommodate the vast crowds attending the various events, the entire festival area had been closed to traffic on the previous evening. My interpreter and I had slipped inside earlier and, after a nap in the street, woke up soon after 4 a.m. to find a long line of Naga *sadhus* standing amid a vast throng of eager pilgrim onlookers. The Naga *sadhus*' mood, calmly unruffled until the day before, had changed, and now, on the brink of the long-awaited sacred bathing, their massed naked, ash-smeared bodies together with their excited squeals in the pre-dawn darkness made for a weird spectacle. I'd been warned not to cut in front of the *sadhus* when I photographed them, but, absorbed in my work, I carelessly did just that, at which I was pummeled mercilessly about the head by several people. The excitement of the *sadhus* was now at its peak. At last, as the sky began to lighten, the crowd set out for the ghats. The parade, to the accompaniment of horns and drums, was underway.

The *sadhus* lined up at the ghat stairways and then, at a signal from their leader, raised a shout and jumped into the water. Shivering with cold, trembling with the joy of washing away the uncleanness in them, they sprinkled their wet bodies with sacred ash. The ash, rising in the air, glowed in the morning sun.

Before coming to India I had photographed Islamic pilgrimages, where I'd seen authorities controlling crowds of two million people – but the Kumbh Mela, in the course of a month, draws multitudes ten times that size from all over the country. And unlike Mecca, where pilgrimages are annual events and a system is in place to accommodate the vast throngs, Ujjain, with its Kumbh Mela every twelve years, seemed a prime candidate for chaos, and it was not without misgivings that I traveled there. One concern among others: would I find a place to stay? As to that at least, I needn't have worried. A travel agency made inquiries for me from Japan, and finding a hotel proved an unexpectedly simple matter.

Nor did the confusion live up to my worst fears. The banks of the Sipra River swarmed with pilgrims, but they were fairly subdued, having walked miles under the blazing sun. The prime culprit in generating chaos is traffic jams, but the impoverished pilgrims of India do not have cars. Many cover the major part of their journeys by train, few paying their fares. There's not much anyone can do about it. Sheer numbers make it impossible to catch and lock up all offenders during a mass displacement such as that generated by the Kumbh Mela. While the festival is in progress, therefore, the authorities resign themselves to winking at violations like non-payment of train fares.

Twilight deepens, and soon not an inch of ground is visible beneath the masses of pilgrims settling down for the night in the open air. Here and there cooking fires flicker. The evening calm is a welcome relief after the intense heat and commotion of the day. In groves and along walls rise mountains of excrement. At Mecca, where bodily purification is required before worship, flush toilets are in place everywhere along the roads pilgrims travel. Not so in India, however.

By the side of the road, cripples and tramps display their sores in an appeal for pity. In developed countries such people are accorded some measure of protection; in India, they are on their own, and must contrive to get their bread by their own efforts. The guide who accompanied me from Delhi tells me that 28.5 percent of all Indians are unable to scrape together three meals a day. Judging by appearances, a good many of the pilgrims here would be among them. What can they do, other than pray to the gods or focus all their hopes on the life to come?

Sadhus and other pilgrims pray and immerse themselves in the holy Sipra River; the Sipra merges into the Yamuna, which at Allahabad meets the Ganges. From its source high in the glaciers of the Himalayas the Ganges flows, limpid at first, growing turbid as it absorbs countless tributaries and swells into a mighty river, stagnating as it ingests the sins and defilements accumulated in the chaotic jostling of everyday life by Indians from every corner of the subcontinent. Corpses, sewage – all impurities find their way into the Ganges as it flows 1550 miles (2500 km) into the Bay of Bengal. The Ganges is India itself. It is the great river of Hinduism, and everything that this vast land has produced over 5000 years is at the last also consumed by it.

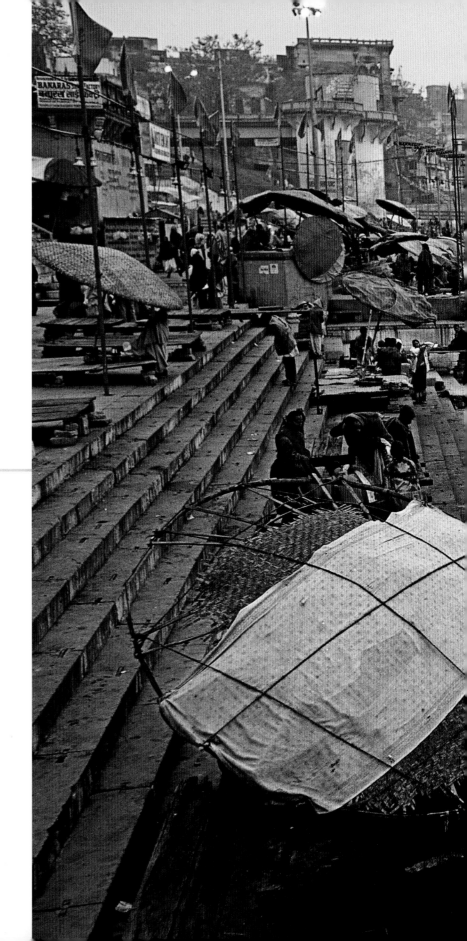

208-209 Dashashwamedh Ghat early in the
morning. In Varanasi, Hinduism's holiest site,
there are no fewer than 60 bathing places
known as ghats.

211 Bathing as the sun rises. To bathe in the Ganges at holy times, it is said, is to wash away all one's sins.

212 A *sadhu*, Hindu ascetic, meditates on the bank of the river. Hinduism is divided into two broad sects – the Shiva sect and the Vishnu sect. *Sadhu*s of the Vishnu sect tend to engage in particularly strict austerities.

213 A *sadhu* paints a "U" on his forehead – symbol of the Vishnu sect.

214-215 A *sadhu* smokes ganja – dried marijuana. The *sadhus* are gathered for the Kumbh Mela held in April 2004 in the holy city of Ujjain in central India. The previous Ujjain Kumbh Mela had been held 12 years earlier.

216 and 216-217 The *puja* ceremony on the riverbank at
Ujjain at sundown. As Brahmins chant mantras and
present their offering of fire, ordinary people too pray.

218 and 218-219 The *puja* ceremony is held at sundown at all
holy places along the Ganges. Photo left was taken at a
Varanasi temple; photo right, by the clear water flowing
through the holy city of Rishikesh, far upstream.

220-221 Women sending the ancestral spirits on their way in Varanasi early
in the morning with *arti* lanterns decked with leaves and flowers.

222 and 222-223 Varanasi *puja*. *Puja* means "worship" in Sanskrit.
The preliminary formality is a milk offering to the Ganges, while onlookers
chant mantras and ring bells.

Kumbh Mela

Sadhus bathing

224-225 The holiest day of the month-long Kumbh
Mela is Shahi Asnan, the kings' bathing day – the
climax of the Kumbh Mela. The *sadhus* begin the
day with an early-morning bath.

226-227 A Kumbh Mela brings together nearly 100,000 *sadhus*. Bathing begins before dawn and continues throughout the morning. After bathing, *sadhus* sprinkle their bodies with holy ashes.

228-229 At 4 a.m. on the day of Shahi Asnan, stark-naked *sadhus* known as *Naga Sadhu* step to the fore, whipping up their spirits in preparation for departure.

ETHIOPIA

THE TRADITIONS
OF THE OLD TESTAMENT

ETHIOPIA

THE TRADITIONS OF THE OLD TESTAMENT

I T WAS TOWARD THE END OF JANUARY 1981 THAT I FIRST VISITED THE HOLY SITE OF LAL-IBELA, KNOWN FOR ITS UNDERGROUND CHURCH-ES DUG DEEP INTO THE BEDROCK.

My original aim had been to photograph the Timqat Festival, held there on January 19, but Ethiopia back then was a closed socialist society; one needed official permission to travel, and that took time. The festival came and went while I cooled my heels in Adis Abeba, the capital. It was a bitter disappointment. It so happened, though, that two days after I arrived Lalibela celebrated Saint Giyorgis' Day, and at the underground cross-shaped church known as Bet Giyorgis there was to be a festival, I was told, similar to Timqat. Somewhat doubtfully, I made my way to the church.

At the appointed time, with throngs of villagers looking on, a horn sounded and a *tabot* was borne out of the stone church on the head of a priest. (A *tabot* is a replica of the stone tablets on which the Ten Commandments were inscribed, given by God to Moses on Mount Sinai as proof of the covenant between them. Every church has one; it is believed to stand for God himself.) The colorfully robed priests of St. Giyorgis formed ranks, a bugle blared, and the procession was underway. The *tabot*, swathed in resplendent brocade, was preceded by a Cross, and behind the *tabot* was carried a painting of Saint Giyorgis on horseback slaying the evil dragon. The crowd swelled as the procession advanced. At the square the priests' dance in honor of the *tabot* began. Each priest held a staff in his left hand and cymbals, known as sistra, in his right. The cymbals clashed in rhythm to the dance. The intoned prayers sounded at first like Japanese Buddhist hymns known as *goeika*. Then the drums joined in, and the fervor mounted, the priests in their bright attire whirling violently. It was a dance such as I had never seen before. This was a culture different from any I'd known. Its survival down the ages in Ethiopia's remote mountain villages was astonishing. Had I been whisked through time into the distant past?

It was only after I returned to Japan that I understood that all this dated back to the reign of King David of Israel 3000 years ago, and was recorded in the Old Testament: "And David and all the house of Israel played before the Lord on all manner of instruments made of fir wood, even on harps, and on psalteries, and on timbrels, and on cornets, and on cymbals." (2 Samuel 6, 5.)

230 Monks at the Debra Damo Monastery.

233 From the Aksum church where the Ark is said to be stored, replicas are brought out on holidays.

Under a clear blue sky, in the mountain foothills, not a power pole in sight, the religious celebration unfolded, the barefoot villagers clad in tribal dress that seemed almost part of their bodies. Among these people, everyday life scarcely differed from what it had been in the times of the Old Testament.

The electric light had yet to penetrate the village of Lalibela, with its rude, somewhat tumbledown houses in the shadow of a mountain slope. In contrast to the shabbiness of the village were the churches dug into the bedrock. Their scale is immense. Nowhere else in the world is there anything quite like this honeycomb of churches fashioned in the depths of the red volcanic rock.

The main church building, carved directly out of the enormous bedrock, is surrounded by a deep, wide courtyard. The church interior – the chancel, the skylight and so on – represents the final stage of construction. There are 11 churches in all, linked by a complex network of underground tunnels. The largest of them, Bet Madhane Alam, is a vast structure, able to accommodate more hundreds worshippers. Scarcely less distinctive is the marvelous exterior of Bet Giyorgis, with its towering cross, 9 ft 9 in. (3 m) high, and its rectangular courtyard.

These churches, dating back to the 12th century, are said to have been built by the Zagwe dynasty, whose ancestors, having lost a battle for royal authority, fled to Jerusalem. They spent five years there before returning and taking the throne, after which they set about constructing at Lalibela "the Jerusalem of Ethiopia." Evidently Jerusalem made a powerful impression on them. Lalibela boasts its own Mount of Olives, Jordan River and Golgotha, names familiar to all readers of the Bible.

On Sunday I went to church at dawn to see Mass. With the villagers I descended the stone stairway. Suddenly rising up from the surrounding darkness came a pitiful chorus of voices. Beggars.

"Sella Mariam, Sella Krestos . . . Mary, Jesus, bless us." Dirty hands reached out to us. The beggars, their survival depending on the sympathy of the believers, had taken shelter from the rain under the eaves of the church. In the darkness of the church interior glowed beeswax candles. The stuffy air was thickened with the fragrance of frankincense, like burning pine resin. At last a heavy drum sounded, and the praying began, the slow tempo reminding me once again of Japanese Buddhist hymns. This was nothing like the refined Christianity of Western Europe. This was rapture rising up from the depths of darkness – the primitive impulse to prayer.

Two architectural styles define Ethiopian churches – rectangular and round. The grotto churches of Lalibela and elsewhere are rectangular, with a sacred space for the *tabot*, set off by a curtain at the extreme rear of the altar. The round churches are adaptations of the round private dwellings seen everywhere in Africa. In round churches there is a circular gallery, in the center of which is a square room, set off by curtains, which houses the *tabot*. All churches require that you remove your shoes before entering. Unlike European churches, where believers are invited to open their hearts, the dimly lit Ethiopian churches foster an unearthly, fearful atmosphere in which the *tabot* is worshipped as an

235 Priests dancing in celebration of Christ's birth as part of the Lalibela Christmas.

incarnation of a stern, unyielding God descended directly from ancient Judaism. Once a friend of mine, a deep believer, said to me, "When I was young I was scared to even go near a church."

During the week before Christmas – the Orthodox Christmas, falling on January 7 – Lalibela swarms with pilgrims, an influx that briefly triples or quadruples the village's permanent population of 8000. Most of the pilgrims I saw came on foot, some from as far away as the Sudan border. The trek through the mountain roads can take as long as two weeks, the pilgrims sleeping outdoors where nightfall happens to find them.

Living at subsistence level in mountain villages, the pilgrims traveled with hardly any cash, cooking as they went the beans and grains they carried with them. Arriving in Lalibela, they gathered on the vacant land near the churches to wait for Christmas Day. Every day their numbers swelled, the crowds thickened. At dusk one could see their cooking fires as they prepared supper. Seen from a distance, it presented a remarkably peaceful spectacle. Their simple meal done, the pilgrims braced themselves against the plateau's evening chill. Wrapping themselves in their thin blankets, they lay themselves down on the rocky ground, entrusting themselves to God's protection as they drifted off to sleep.

They were up before dawn, making the rounds of Lalibela's 11 churches.

Following tradition, they stood in the church entrance, removing their sandals (if they were not, as most were, barefoot to begin with) and seeking divine grace by kissing the church pillars and stroking their own bodies with hands that had touched the church walls. When they encountered a priest in the street they asked to be permitted to worship the cross. The priest would then remove a cross from the folds of his robe, and the pilgrims would reverently kiss it and press their foreheads against it.

Day after day, crowds of pilgrims lined up to attend the prayer rituals at the various churches. Beggars thronged the roads, pleading to votaries for alms.

The votaries, scarcely better dressed than the beggars, nonetheless doled out small change. It is their way of accepting their share of the world's suffering. Monks in rough garments appeared, and began their street preaching. To be in Lalibela at such a time is find oneself in scenes straight out of the Bible.

At the center of the network of churches is Bet Mariam (St. Mary's Church), and here, on the day before Christmas, prayers in praise of God and the priests' dances began.

The hymns with their monotonous melodies, and the dancing went on, with intermittent pauses for rest, right through the night of Christmas Eve.

At daybreak the pilgrims streamed into Bet Mariam. Crosses and portraits of Mary and the infant Christ were raised high over the walls surrounding the church. Women, thousands of them, shouted for joy. The excitement of Christmas was at its peak when about eighty priests, dressed in robes of deep red and pure white, formed a line on the stone wall and began a dance of benediction in celebration of the birth of Christ. The ragged pilgrims gazed at the spectacle with enchanted faces. Standing among them, I myself felt as if the celestial dance was about to soar above the earth and vanish into the blue sky.

The holiest occasion of the Ethiopian Orthodox Church calendar is the Timqat Festival, commemorating the baptism of Jesus in the Jordan River.

The festival is celebrated on January 19. The day before, *tabots* from all the churches are carried in procession to a tent set up beside a spring. The *tabots* are enshrined in the tent, and believers come to offer up their prayers.

On Timqat morning, the priests sanctify the water in a pond and immerse their crosses in it. Frenzied believers rush to the pond. By bathing in it, they participate in Jesus' baptism. This is Timqat's climax.

Generally speaking, *tabots* are replicas of the stone tablets bearing the Ten Commandments, but at Aksum, a town some 150 miles (250 km) north of Lalibela, it is the Ark, the sacred container God ordered Moses to construct for the tablets, rather than the tablets themselves, whose replica is featured in the festival.

The Ark, its loss more deeply felt by ancient Jews than even the loss of the Jerusalem Temple 3000 years ago, was, Ethiopians firmly believe, brought to Ethiopia, where it is housed to this day in a cellar of the church at Aksum. Ethiopian oral tradition has it that the Queen of Sheba, whose visit to King Solomon in Jerusalem is recorded in the Old Testament's *Book of Kings*, was in fact the Queen of Aksum, and that the child she had by Solomon subsequently traveled to Jerusalem and carried off the Ark from the Temple, leaving a counterfeit one in its place. His descendents are believed to be the black Ethiopian Jews known as Falasha – a word meaning "emigrant" in the ancient Ethiopian language. The Falasha live in the mountains of northern Ethiopia. They were said to number some 50,000 until, beginning in 1984, the Israeli army undertook a vast rescue and resettlement operation, airlifting most of them to Israel.

Ethiopians see the glory of God reflected in the Ark brought here by the son of King Solomon and the Queen of Sheba. In a labyrinth beneath a small chapel next to the Mariam of Zion Church, which stages a brilliant procession for its *tabot*, is enshrined the true Ark, believed to be a sign of the manifestation of God. Only one man is permitted to lay eyes on it, a watchman-priest who must not let it out of his sight for so much as an instant. When he dies the responsibility passes to his successor. Latching on to one aged priest, I tried to question him about the Ark, but his silence on the subject was not to be breached. It was not permitted to speak about it, he said, and that was that.

Hidden in the mountains of Tigray (Tigre) Province in northern Ethiopia are countless grotto churches, many of them isolated on precipices like hawks' nests. By climbing rocks and ascending ropes one reach them after a difficult descent.

I had known about these grotto churches before, but following Ethiopia's socialist revolution in 1974, Tigray was seized by the anti-government guerilla Tigray Liberation Front, and throughout the ensuing civil war, a fierce and protracted conflict, the territory was off-limits to foreigners. I visited Ethiopia often during the 1980s, but Tigray was like some eternal, inaccessible illusion. Then the Cold War ended, Ethiopia lost its Soviet protection, and the socialist regime crumbled. By 1991 anti-government guerillas were in control of the whole country. The civil war ended, and three years later it became possible to travel to Tigray. In 1996 I finally as able to reach those mountain churches I had dreamed of seeing for so long.

Ravaged by repeated droughts, reeling from the long civil war, Tigray was a near wasteland when I arrived. Whenever I saw an abandoned tank or artillery piece belonging to the former government – the fields and roadsides were littered with them – I thought of the million or so people said to have starved while the war was at its height in 1984-85. The price of just one of those tanks could have saved many lives.

Scattered here and there through northern Ethiopia are lava plateaus, isolated by erosion from the surrounding landscape and looking like so many desert islands. Hidden away in these plateaus and in vertical precipices are numerous natural caves. Before Christianity came to Ethiopia in the 4th century AD, worship in caves had been a flourishing tradition. Perhaps under its influence, early Christians dug their own mountain cave-churches, elaborating in each a spacious inner temple.

A ninety-minute walk along a precipitous path brought me to the Debra Abuna Aron monastery ("debra" means monastery) at the edge of one of those desert island-like plateaus. The monastery, set in a thicket of tall grass, presented a rather forlorn appearance, its five ramshackle thatch-roofed huts accommodating all of four monks.

The gnarled cypress and olive trees scattered here and there might have been a thousand years old. Red and green birds of a sort rarely seen in the Ethiopian plateau, their coloring so vivid as to seem almost artificial, flitted about the weirdly twisted branches under the glaring sun. Peace reigned supreme. The graceful charm of the scene suggested a deserted and forgotten Eden.

I wanted to see the cave church, I told the monks. Wait until afternoon prayers, they said. Lunch was served in one of the huts. The monks pressed food on me, a kind of ground, fermented cereal called *enjera*. Warily, I tried it, but its extreme sourness was more than I could stomach. My first taste was my last.

The church was set some 33 ft (10 m) inside a natural cave. One of the monks was totally blind, but evidently he knew his way around, and negoti-

ated the dark stone chamber with ease, while I groped uncertainly behind him. Fragrant incense burned. The flames of beeswax candles augmented the dim light that entered through a hole cut in the ceiling. Prayers began, the monks reading from large Bibles, The Bibles were of parchment, and the writing in them was by hand. Hundreds of years of use had left them blackened with finger marks.

Ten minutes passed, and suddenly the church was filled with brightness as sunlight poured through the hole in the ceiling, lighting up the Bibles' timeworn parchment. The monks' voices rose, throbbing with uncontainable fervor. The light lingered for fifteen minutes, then, like a dramatic effect that has served its purpose, faded, and the church returned to its original dimness.

Prayers over, the monks' faces expressed the peace of souls that have been touched by God. The monks say that however violently it rains outside, not a drop of rain ever gets in through the hole in the ceiling. A flashlight lighting our way, we followed a labyrinthine path into the depths of the grotto. Here and there, in hollows in the rocks, lay bleached skeletons clad in rags – dead monks laid to rest. Such is the fate of people who shut themselves off from the outside world to hear the voice of God. In what form, I wondered, does God reveal Himself to them?

Poverty, starvation, tribal wars. . . . Since Genesis, little has changed in this long-suffering land. Reality here is layered, compounded of the deep darkness of everyday life – and the joy is found only in prayer.

239 A priest enters the church's Maqdes, the Holy of Holies, where the *tabot* is enshrined.
To the left and right are pictures of winged angels.

240-241 This nun entered her mountain convent 30 years ago and has not descended the mountain since. The terrain as far as the eye can see has been ravaged by drought and civil war.

242-243 Abba Yohannes Church, dug into a vertical precipice in Tigray Province. The underground tunnel leading into the church's interior is at upper left.

244-245 There's only one way to get to Debre Damo, one of Ethiopia's oldest monasteries, and that's by ascending a 15-meter precipice with the aid of a knitted cowhide rope suspended from the top.

246-247 Church bells made from
basalt stone. Most old mountain
churches have them. The sound varies
depending on the shape of the stone.

Monks hear the voice of God in the wind

249 In northern Ethiopia's Tigray Province, in the mountains far from human habitation, ascetics spend their days immersed in their austere practices, the better to hear the voice of God.

251 Sixty kilometers southwest of Lalibela is the remote bedrock church known as Debre Abuna Aron, its gloomy interior brightened for a mere 15 minutes a day when, just after 1 p.m., a streak of sunlight pours in through a hole in the ceiling.

252-253 This blind monk at the Debre Abuna Aron
monastery had no trouble making his way with
perfect freedom around the darkened grotto.

253 A monk fasting and praying during the "main
fast" of the 55 days before Easter.

254-255 Priests intone their slow-tempo
hymns in Lalibela church grottoes.

256 A medieval painted fan. This fan,
made of over 30 pieces of parchment,
depicts the Virgin Mary, the Twelve
Apostles and other Biblical personalities.

257 Abna Yemata Church, with its
depictions of the Twelve Apostles and
other saints. Abna Yemata is a bedrock
church dug into a vertical precipice 100
meters high.

258-259 This 18th-century work
depicting the Trinity shows the
Father and Son as identical elderly
men and the Holy Ghost as a dove.

260-261 Monks at the Debra Damo
Monastery praying during the "main
fast." For 55 days prior to Easter the
clergy eat only one simple meal a day,
at just after 3 p.m.

LALIBELA
THE JERUSALEM OF AFRICA

262

262-263 In the holy city of Lalibela, with its 11
bedrock churches, place names are straight
out of the Bible – the Mount of Olives, the
Jordan River and Golgotha.

264-265 Monks deliver sermons to a
crowd of Christmas pilgrims. At this time
of year wandering monks converge on
Lalibela, swelling the influx of pilgrims.

266-267 Priests dancing in honor of the
tabot – slowly at first, frenzied at last, to
the fevered rhythm of drums.

268-269 People throng the stone walls surrounding Lalibela's Bet Giorgis (St. George's Church) to hear the preaching of the priests.

270-271 During the Timqat Festival in Addis Ababa, *tabots* are carried from their churches to a public square. The *tabots* are lodged for the night in a tent, then returned the following day to the churches.

272-273 *Tabots* swathed in colorful cloth are brought out of their churches, borne on the heads of priests. *Tabots* are to be neither seen nor touched except by authorized priests.

274-275 and 275 The faithful look on as priests dance in praise of the *tabot* on its return to Bet Giorgis, a church cut out of the rock in the shape of a cross.

276-277 A woman who bathes in the church courtyard pond on the day before Christmas will be blessed with a child, according to local belief. Clutching a lifeline, this woman plunges into the algae-choked water.

278 This pilgrim arrived in Lalibela after a week's trek along mountain roads. At night he slept in the open.

279 This female pilgrim, a cross tatooed on her forehead, came from a farming village in the northern part of the country.

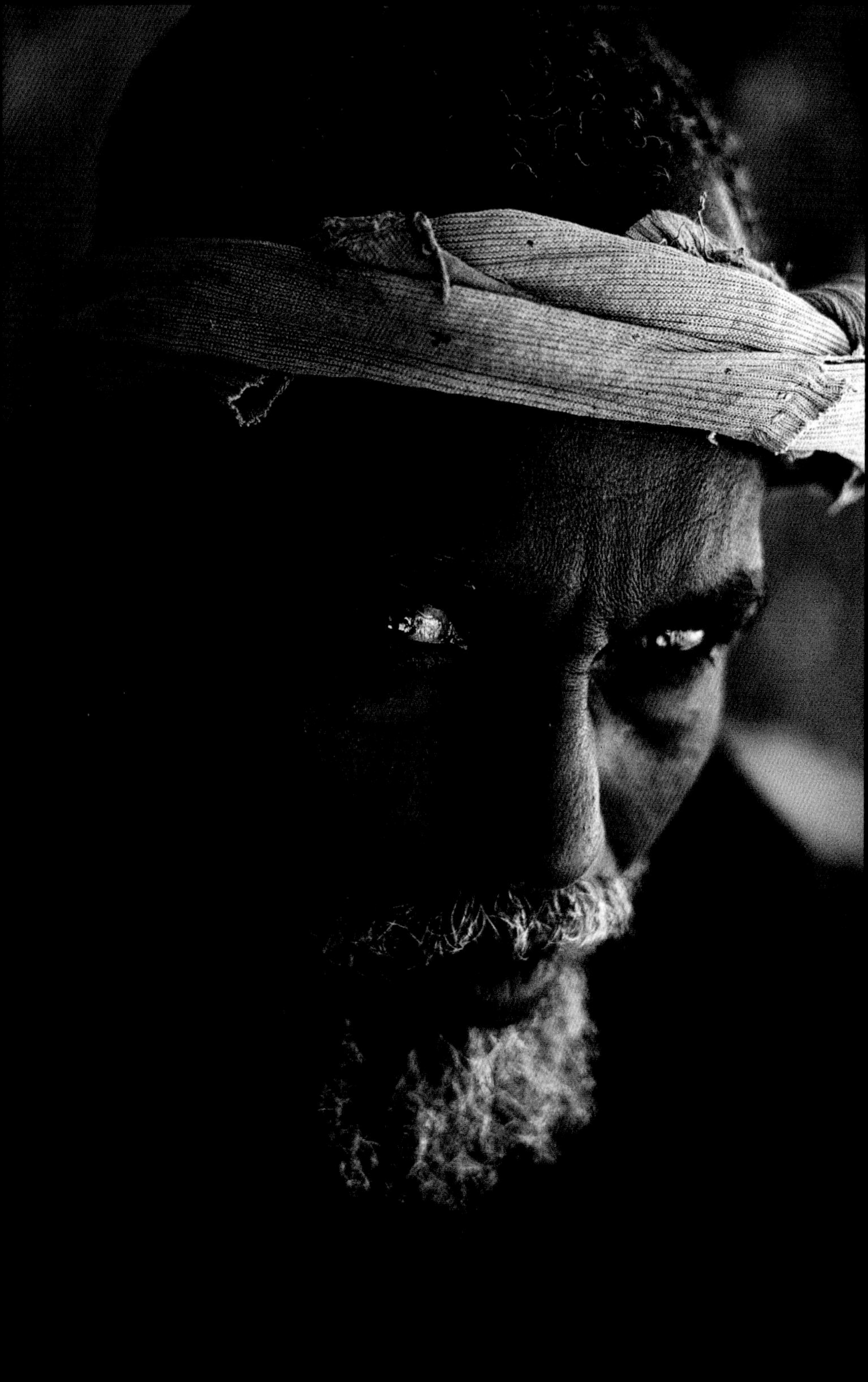

280 Christmas pilgrims huddle close to a church wall as they pray. Window-like openings in church walls are arranged in various patterns to form decorative crosses.

280-281 The stone wall behind the woman prostrating herself in prayer is said to be the grave of mankind's first ancestor, Adam.

282-283 and 283 On Christmas morning, after receiving the priests'
blessings, the pilgrims form long lines along the roads leaving home.
Some among them – those living in villages near the Sudan border –
will be on the road for two weeks, sleeping in the open.

THE RAINS
CAME TOO LATE

BLACK CLOUDS HUNG OVER THE ETHIOPIAN PLATEAU. THE RAINY SEASON HAD ARRIVED. FOR THREE TORTURED, DROUGHT-STRICKEN YEARS THE PEOPLE HAD WAITED FOR IT — WAITED FOR A SIGN THAT THE BLESSED RAIN WOULD FALL. HERE IT WAS AT LAST — TOO LATE.

Starvation gripped the land like an endemic disease. Mountain peasants endured as best they could, eating weeds and tree bark. Some villagers who lived close enough to a main road took their straw-thatch huts apart, stacked the debris by the roadside and sold it as firewood. At word of a shelter opening somewhere, people abandoned their villages and flocked to the towns. Refugees in rags were every-where, spreading turmoil and confusion.

For them, penniless as they were, the violent squalls peculiar to Ethiopia at this time of year were a curse, a death rain. Hordes of them took shelter in makeshift huts hardly sturdy enough to keep out the cold rain. Children, debilitated by their ordeals, succumbed one after another to the epidemic diseases that spread so easily.

A million people are said to have starved to death, most of them children.

They died like insects at the turn of the season. Exhausted by their long struggle against hunger, those not yet dead were too feeble to muster even despair. As I watched their faces through my viewfinder it came home to me, not for the first time, how utterly fragile a thing life is.

287 Starved, exhausted, crushed by life, the people can scarcely muster the energy to brush away the buzzing flies.

288-289 A young girl watches helplessly over
her sick mother. Many, many children die – and
many more are orphaned when their parents die.

291 Under a merciless noon sun, a mother and daughter join
a long line of people waiting for medical attention.

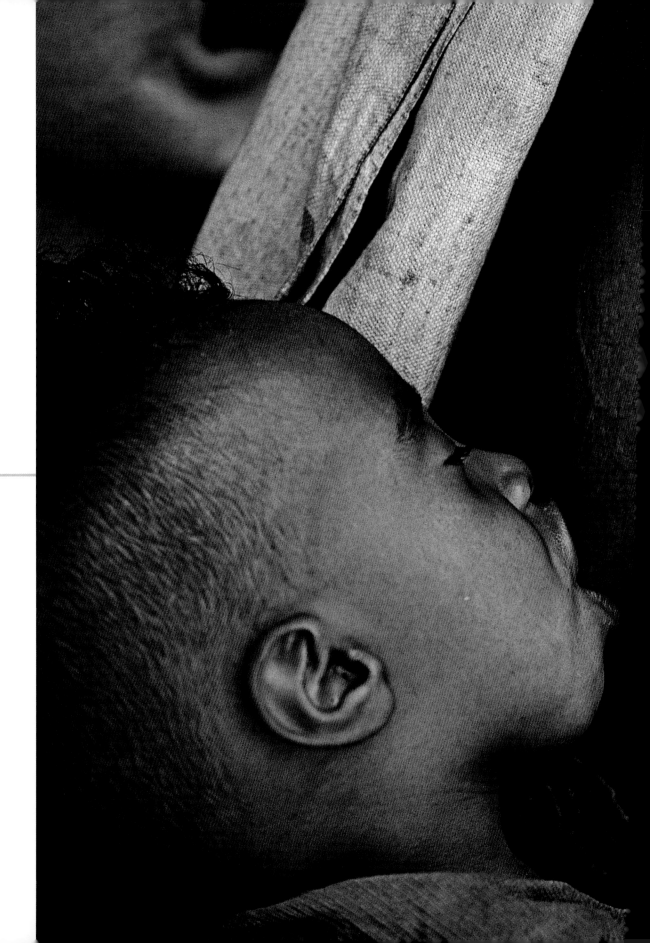

292-293 A mother with
twins waits for food
rations. Food shortage
remains a problem in
Ethiopia to this day, and
starvation looms
whenever the rains fail.

THE HOLIEST CITIES OF ISLAM

MECCA AND MEDINA

THE POLES OF THE ISLAMIC UNIVERSE

MECCA AND MEDINA

THE POLES OF THE ISLAMIC UNIVERSE

Nothing could have been more unexpected. In the course of a lifetime spent traveling and giving my curiosity free rein, I had seen a good deal of the world, but Mecca, sacred city of Islam, seemed irrevocably off-limits.

Then, in October 1994, came the invitation I could never have imagined myself receiving – from a Saudi Arabian I had never met.

In the year AD 610 God revealed Himself to a Mecca merchant named Muhammad, and the religion known as Islam was born. On Muhammad's instructions, access to Islam's two holiest sites, Mecca and Medina, was eternally forbidden to unbelievers. Thus veiled, the two cities have naturally, down the ages, aroused considerable curiosity among non-Muslims – curiosity that for the most part had to go unsatisfied. Some unbelievers converted to Islam; others merely pretended to, risking their lives to gain entry to the holy sites. Down the centuries they have left precious records of their impressions.

Beginning in the Sahara, my travels from East Africa to Central Asia have taken me through a wide swath of Islamic territory, but Mecca and Medina, the centers of the Islamic universe, were beyond the reach of my cameras.

The Saudi Arabian who contacted me was in the process of starting a publishing company. It was Medina, not Mecca, he was interested in to begin with. His plan was to produce a book of photographs of Medina, and he hoped to enlist me as the photographer. He had seen some of my photo anthologies published in Europe, and decided I was the man for the job. How could I, a non-Muslim, enter the city? I asked. I was not to worry, he said; he had already obtained the informal consent of the authorities. Only the interiors of the mosques would be closed to me.

If Medina, I thought to myself, why not Mecca? Was it possible? If so, it would be a dream come true – a chance at last to photograph a Mecca pilgrimage! For that, though, I would have convert to Islam.

Extensive travel in Muslim lands had familiarized me with the Islamic religious worldview. Its one-to-one God-to-man relationship was not uncongenial to me. Not without some doubts all the same, I nonetheless went through the formalities at

297　Pilgrims perform *Tawaf,* walking counterclockwise round the Kaaba and stretching out their hands in prayer to the Kaaba's golden door.

the Islamic Center in Setagaya, Tokyo. These involve chanting, in Arabic, a profession of faith: "La ilaha ill-Allah, there is no God but Allah; Muhammad-ur-rasool-ullah, Muhammad is Allah's apostle."

That done, I departed for Saudi Arabia in January 1995. Jeddah, gateway to Mecca and Medina, proudly displays the prosperity befitting an oil-producing country. Four years after the Persian Gulf War, calm was returning, but the war was still very much on people's minds. "Wasn't it America that built Saddam Hussein up into a dictator nobody could touch? They used him to seal off Iran." Such was the general view in Saudi Arabia. The popular perception was that the Gulf War gave the U.S. its opportunity to permanently station its military here with a view toward controlling Arabian oil. The Arab masses' seething hatred of the U.S. would explode six years later on 9/11.

In my more than 30 years as a photographer, one scene above all others has left its indelible impression on my brain: that of a million people worshipping through the night of Laylat al-Qadr. It was the month of Ramadan, 1995. From my perch atop a minaret towering 316 ft (96 m) over the Mecca mosque, I watched as the human mass formed concentric circles around the Kaaba shrine and then, at the mullah's shout "Allah akbar, God is great," prostrated themselves as one, while I, still standing, found myself shuddering with fear at the thought that I had arrogated to myself a vantage point to which God alone was entitled.

The guard who had escorted me to the top of the minaret went down again, leaving me to myself.

Alone, I gazed at the worshipping multitude. The mullah's voice, as though possessed by some supernatural force, resounded sonorously in the night air. One thing I was convinced of: that this scene I was witnessing represented a climax of mankind's spiritual journey; that never since the dawn of humanity had there been a more complete, more absolute submission to God.

Laylat al-Qadr means "night of power," or "night of the decree." It commemorates the night God appeared to Muhammad as Muhammad meditated in a cave atop Mount Hillah in the outskirts of Mecca. It was a revelation of such force as to transform this Mecca merchant into a prophet of the one God. Muhammad was then 40 years old. It was the year 610 of the Christian calendar, the night of the 27th day of the month of Ramadan.

To worship at the sacred mosque on the night of Laylat al-Qadr is said to be the equivalent of 1000 months of prayer. On this night, therefore, pilgrims descend upon Mecca from all over the world. Entering the mosque, the pilgrims first perform *Tawaf*, the walk round the holy Kaaba sanctuary. Beginning at the sacred black stone housed in the southeast angle of the sanctuary and proceeding counter-clockwise, they walk around the Kaaba seven times, a formality obligatory for all believers. (Buddhist processions, incidentally, proceed clockwise.)

The Kaaba, Muslims believe, is the very center of the universe, located on the axis linking earth to heaven. Covered with black cloth, it is, in a manner of speaking, a black hole. Its role in Islam is unique

and irreplaceable. Every day 1.2 billion Muslims, wherever in the world they may be, worship facing the Kaaba. If they are in Asia, they face west; if in Africa, east. On this night of Laylat al Qadr, Muslims in every corner of the Islamic world worship through the night, focusing their intense prayers on the Kaaba, that they may rise to Allah in heaven.

Islamic oral tradition has it that the Kaaba was built by Ibrahim (Abraham), servant of the one God, together with his son Ishmael. Time passed, mankind grew depraved, and Mecca turned into a pantheon for the worship of many gods, with 360 idols enshrined in the Kaaba. Muhammad, victorious in battle, smashed the idols and returned the Kaaba to Allah. The Kaaba has been a symbol ever since of faith in the one God. Though regarded as a religion directly descended from Judaism and Christianity, its monotheistic progenitors, Islam insists on identifying its origins with Abraham (Ibrahim). Judaism, Muslims say, degenerated into a closed, tribal faith, while Christianity, in embracing the doctrine of the Trinity, lost its right to be considered a religion of the one God.

Allah is a transcendent being beyond the reach of the human imagination. Embodying Him in images is strictly forbidden. Thus the interior of the Kaaba is, for all eternity, empty space.

Twice a year the gold doors of the Kaaba are opened, and a ceremonial purification is performed. Dignitaries, including the governor of Mecca province as representative of the king, enter the Kaaba and clean the interior. I myself was on this one occasion permitted to enter. The sanctuary is of pure white marble, absolutely stainless. Inside, three circular golden pillars support the ceiling. Near the ceiling, wire stretches from pillar to pillar. From the wire are suspended golden jars of fragrant oil.

For 1400 years nothing in here has disturbed the flow of time and space. In Islam, devoted as it is to an eternal transcendent being, time has two components only: eternity, and the present moment.

The all night prayer vigil of Laylat al-Qadr ends with prayers to see in the dawn. As the sky in the east lightened, unveiling the craggy contours of Mount Hillah 3 miles (ca. 5 km) away, the pilgrims, having completed their prayers, gathered round the Kaaba for *Tawaf.* The swelling human wave revolved around the Kaaba, unmoving center of the Islamic universe, like the Milky Way pursuing its course through space. Then the Kaaba, as if infused with the energy of the *Tawaf,* seemed itself to cast off its earthly bonds and soar into celestial orbit.

March 26, 1999. Dawn breaks over the tents in the Valley of Mina, on the outskirts of Mecca. By the Muslim calendar it is the second month of the year 1419, the time of the great annual pilgrimage known as the *hajj.*

The climax of the *hajj* is the Day of Arafat.

It's just past 4:30 a.m., and already the two million temporary inhabitants of this tent village are awake. Under glaring street lamps the giant human wave begins to move toward Arafat. Half are on foot, the others in vehicles jammed bumper to bumper. Bells ring. Arafat is about 8 miles (13 km) ahead. The flow of humanity seems endless. Voices rise up in chorus, chanting the words to the Tardiya prayer:

"Labbaik Allahumma labbaik. . . . O Allah, we will serve You. . . ."

On this day, the pilgrims gather on vacant land in Arafat and pray to God for forgiveness of their sins. "*Uuquf,*" it's called – the most important event of the *hajj.* Anyone who fails to participate in this rite is not recognized as having completed the *hajj.* In Arafat stands the granite Mount Rahmah (Mountain of Mercy). By sunrise the pilgrims are swarming up the mountain, like ants. At the summit towers a white pillar. In AD 653 the prophet Muhammad, sensing that his life was nearing its end, undertook a "pilgrimage of parting," and at this place, before 100,000 of his followers, delivered the sermon that came to be known as the Sermon of Parting:

"Know," he said, "that all Muslims are brothers, that you are all as one. If there is any superiority or inferiority among you, it concerns only the degree of your reverence for God."

With that, his prophetic mission was concluded, and Islam, he declared, was complete. The present-day *hajj* is a faithful recreation of the pilgrimage of parting.

Prior to the *hajj,* pilgrims must shed all clothing and accessories suggestive of individual identity or character. After purifying their persons by bathing in designated places, they don a two-piece seamless white cloth garment known as an *ihlam.* They replace their shoes with rubber sandals. Shorn of all artificial attributes, they are now ready to face God one to one. Confessing their sins, they cling to God's mercy and beg His forgiveness. On this day the pilgrims gathered at Arafat, clad in *ihlam,* lined up in rows and praying together, transcend race, language and social status; they renew their sense of being members of one community, the community of Islam.

The donning of the *ihlam* symbolizes that the wearer has entered into a state of abstinence in which shedding blood, conflict and sexual relations are strictly taboo. Quarrelling of any kind during the pilgrimage is forbidden. The *ihlam* is also a Muslim's death garment. After the pilgrimage, the pilgrim takes his *ihlam* home. One day it will cover his naked corpse, stripped by death of all personal attributes. He will be buried with it, and with it he will return, naked, into the arms of Allah.

A believer departing on a pilgrimage must first settle all debts. In past ages a pilgrimage meant joining up with a caravan and crossing the Arabian desert; the pilgrim could not be sure of coming back alive, and personal affairs had to be put in order beforehand. Today, when most pilgrims simply hop on a plane, the uncertainty is much reduced, but the obligation remains in force.

The pilgrims leave Arafat at sundown. They pause for a nap at Muzdalifah, midway between Arafat and Mina. There also they collect pebbles for use in the stone-throwing ceremony at Mina. Between midnight and dawn they resume their journey. Their destination is the land-bridge at Mina known as Jamarat. The bridge rests on three stone pillars. On this day it is the pillar called Aqaba the stone-throwers will target. The ceremony symbolizes the Muslim's determination to overcome evil temptation. Owing to the danger presented by the intense crush, old people and women are permitted to appoint substitutes. In fact, every year here more than a few pilgrims are trampled to death.

After the stone-throwing the pilgrims cut their hair as a sign that they have completed the pilgrimage. The majority cut only an obligatory lock, but nearly half the men shave their heads. Then the meat from the sacrificial beasts – the actual slaughtering is done nowadays by professional slaughterers in Muzdalifah – is distributed among the pilgrims. The festival of which this is the central observance is called *Id al-adha*, Festival of Sacrifice. Islam's biggest festival, it marks the end of the *hajj*. All over the Islamic world households sacrifice livestock in its honor. The pilgrims spend two days in the tent village at Mina and then, on the twelfth day of the pilgrimage, leave Mina before sundown. At the Kaaba there is one last *Tawafa*, the *Tawafa* of parting, before the final departure from Mecca.

Engaging in trade to cover the cost of the pilgrimage is by no means frowned upon. In the old days, when caravans gathered from all over the Islamic world, pilgrimage and trade were inseparable. That remains true today, to some extent. Women pilgrims from Southeast Asia sell large quantities of imitation accessories; a lively commerce in cheap Persian carpets and Russian cameras is another familiar backdrop to the *hajj*.

Pilgrims at Mina bask in the fulfillment of a life-long desire. The newly fledged *hajjis* – believers who have completed the pilgrimage – are filled with a sense of liberation. Before, wrapped in their *ihlams*, they felt the tension of an individual face to face with Allah; now they are back in their native dress, in their best clothes for *Id al-adha*. Gazing upon the vast Mina tent village, I am struck once again by the variety of nationalities brought together here, the many different styles of dress a glittering reflection of Islam's diversity.

Having converged upon Mecca from all over the world and reaffirmed Islam's core solidarity, the pilgrims will now return to their several countries. The three million people – at the very least – who take part in the pilgrimages of the month of Ramadan and the lesser, optional pilgrimages, are participants in a cycle of convergence and dispersion that year after year confirms the fundamental unity of the Islamic world. Thus is Islam regenerated and spread. To put it another way, Mecca, in the 1400 years since Islam's birth, is the heart which pumps fresh blood to all corners of the community of believers. Being part of the pilgrimage has raised my awareness both of the vast extent of the Islamic world and of Mecca as that world's only sacred site. The Islamic community today embraces no less than one-sixth of the world's population.

303 Women reciting the prayers of sunset at the Mosque of the Prophet in Medina take up every inch of available space.

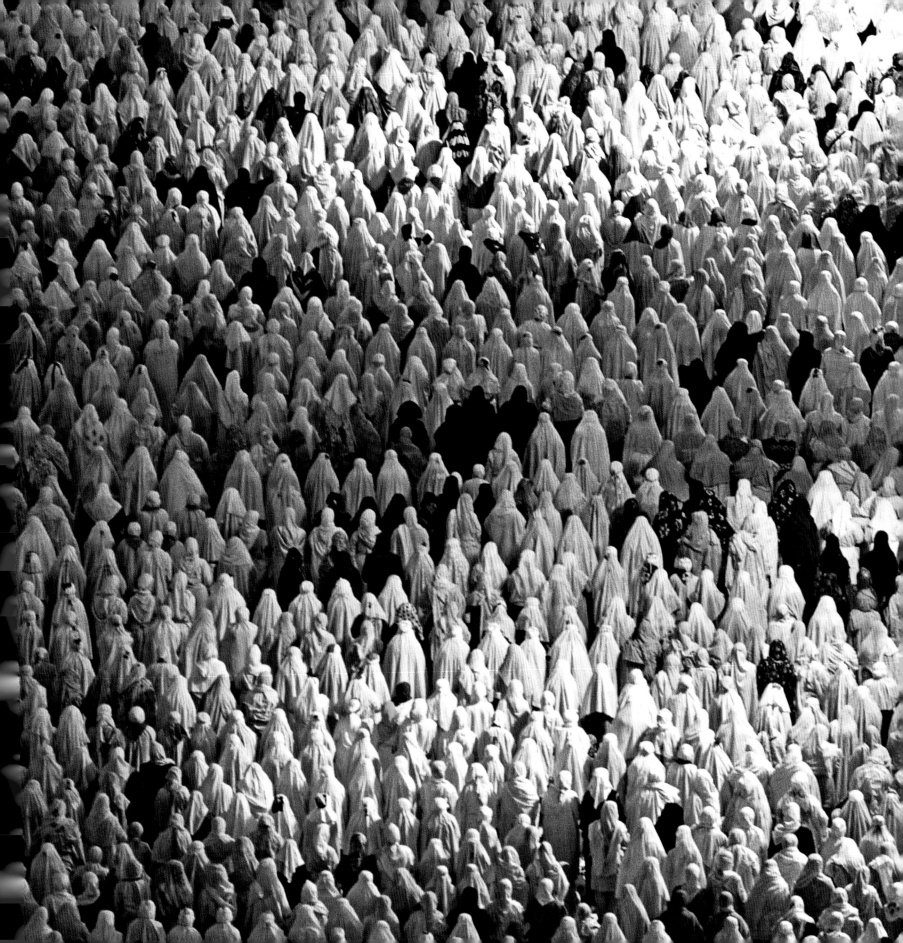

Mecca

Two million people at the *Hajj*.

304-305 Two pilgrims lingering on a hill
overlooking the tent village at Mina. Pilgrims spend
five days in the tent village.

306-307 Pilgrims from
Pakistan await the start
of prayers on the grounds
of the holy mosque.
In Haram all quarreling is
strictly forbidden.

308 Embroidering the *Kiswah* by hand using gold threads at a factory in Mecca.

309 A number of pilgrims are accorded the special honor of standing before the door of the Kaaba in prayer.

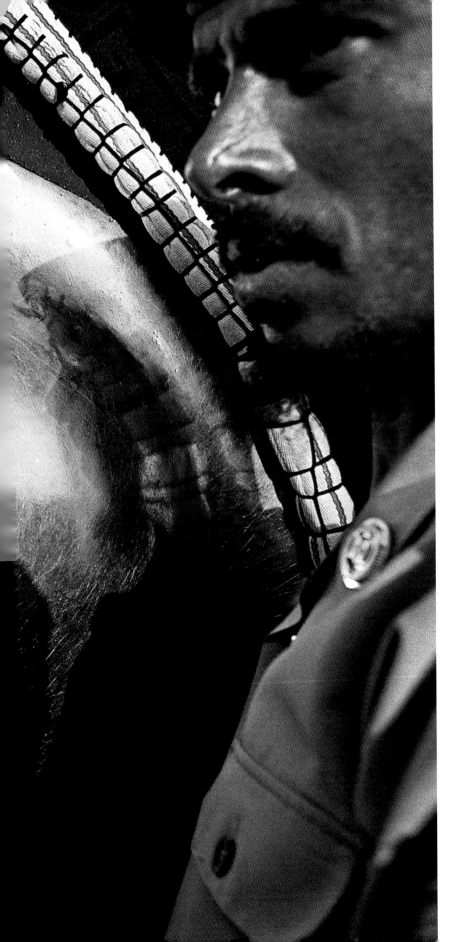

310-311 The Black Stone is believed by Muslims to have descended from heaven as the symbol of the covenant between God and Adam and Adam's progeny.

313 A pilgrim stretches out his hand to the *Kiswah*, the black cloth covering the Kaaba, as he prays. He is clad in an *ihram* – pilgrims' attire composed of two strips of white cloth.

314-315 A pilgrim couple from Pakistan rest their heads against the *Kiswah* as they pray. The *Kiswah*, made from strips of black woven silk cloth, is replaced once a year, on the ninth day of the month of pilgrimage.

316-317 Pilgrims have their hair cut as a sign they have completed the *hajj*. Women cut only a ceremonial lock or two, but most men have their heads shaved.

318-319 Maghrib prayers at sunset in the tent village in Mina. One series of regulations concerning pilgrimages, dating from the time of Muhammad, enjoins believers to follow the route taken by the Prophet and his followers in the year 632.

321 A man is moved to tears as the *hajj* moves into its climax. To a
Muslim, visiting Mecca is the equivalent of fulfilling a promise to God.

322-323 The night of the 27th day of
the month of Ramadan is the holiest
night of the Muslim year, for on that
night the Quran was first revealed to
the prophet Muhammad.

324-325 Laylat al-Qadr prayers
continue through the night. Pilgrims
performing *Tawaf* walk seven times
counter-clockwise around the Kaaba.

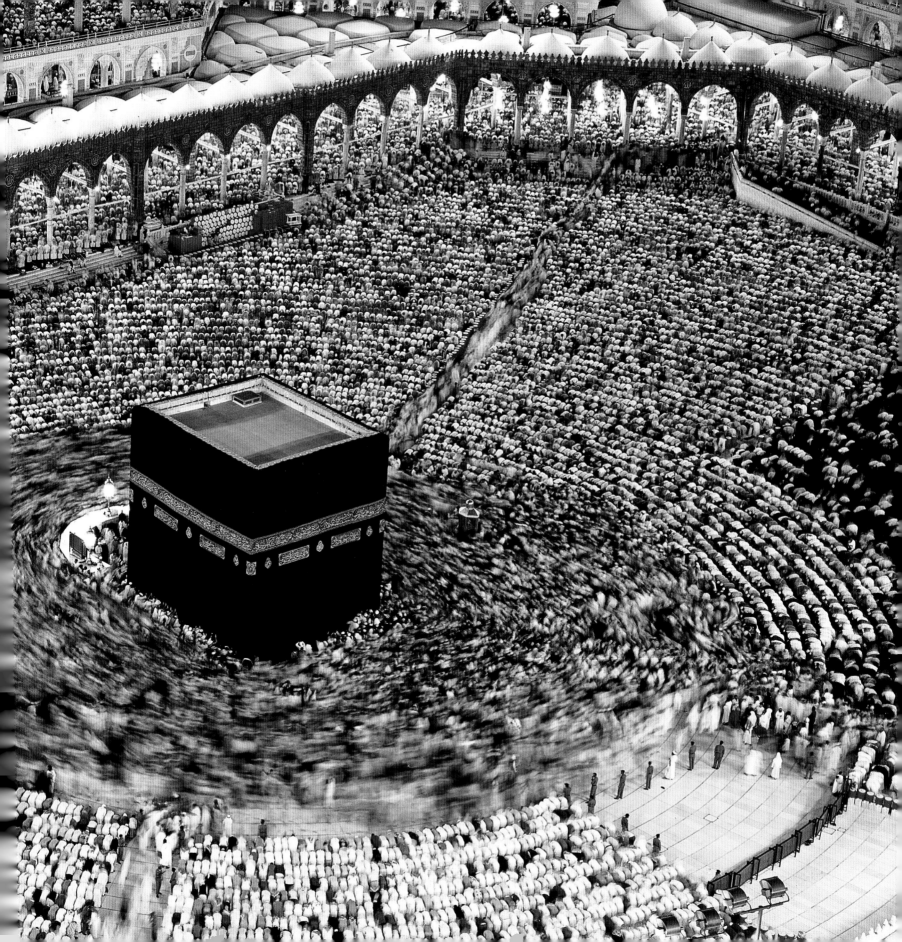

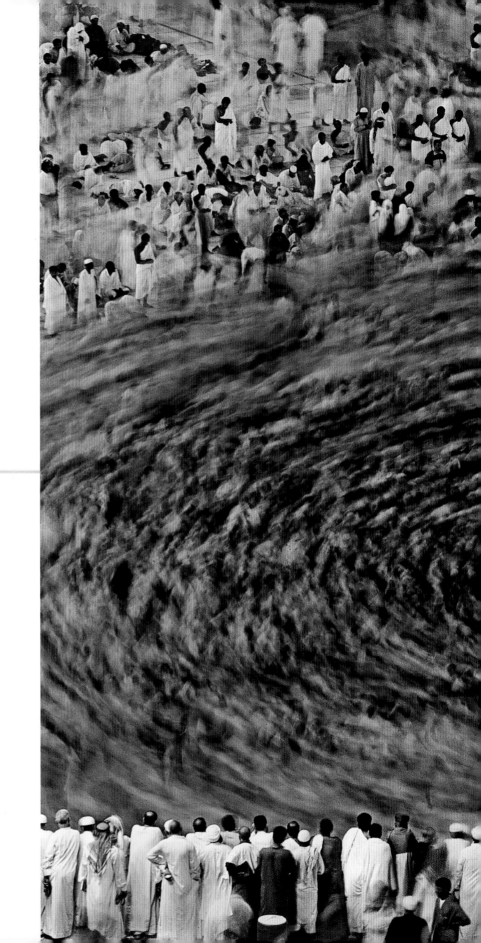

326-327 During a pause in prayers, the *Tawaf*
around the Kaaba resembles a giant whirlpool
as people look on from roof tops.

MEDINA

ISLAM'S SECOND HOLIEST CITY

328-329 The Mosque of the Prophet is built around Muhammad's tomb, which lies beneath the green domes at the center of the mosque. Shown here are morning prayers for Id al-Fitr, the festival that ends the Ramadan fast.

331 A pilgrim from Nigeria praying by the door of the Mosque of the Prophet. Pilgrims to
Mecca include Medina in their itinerary as a matter of course.

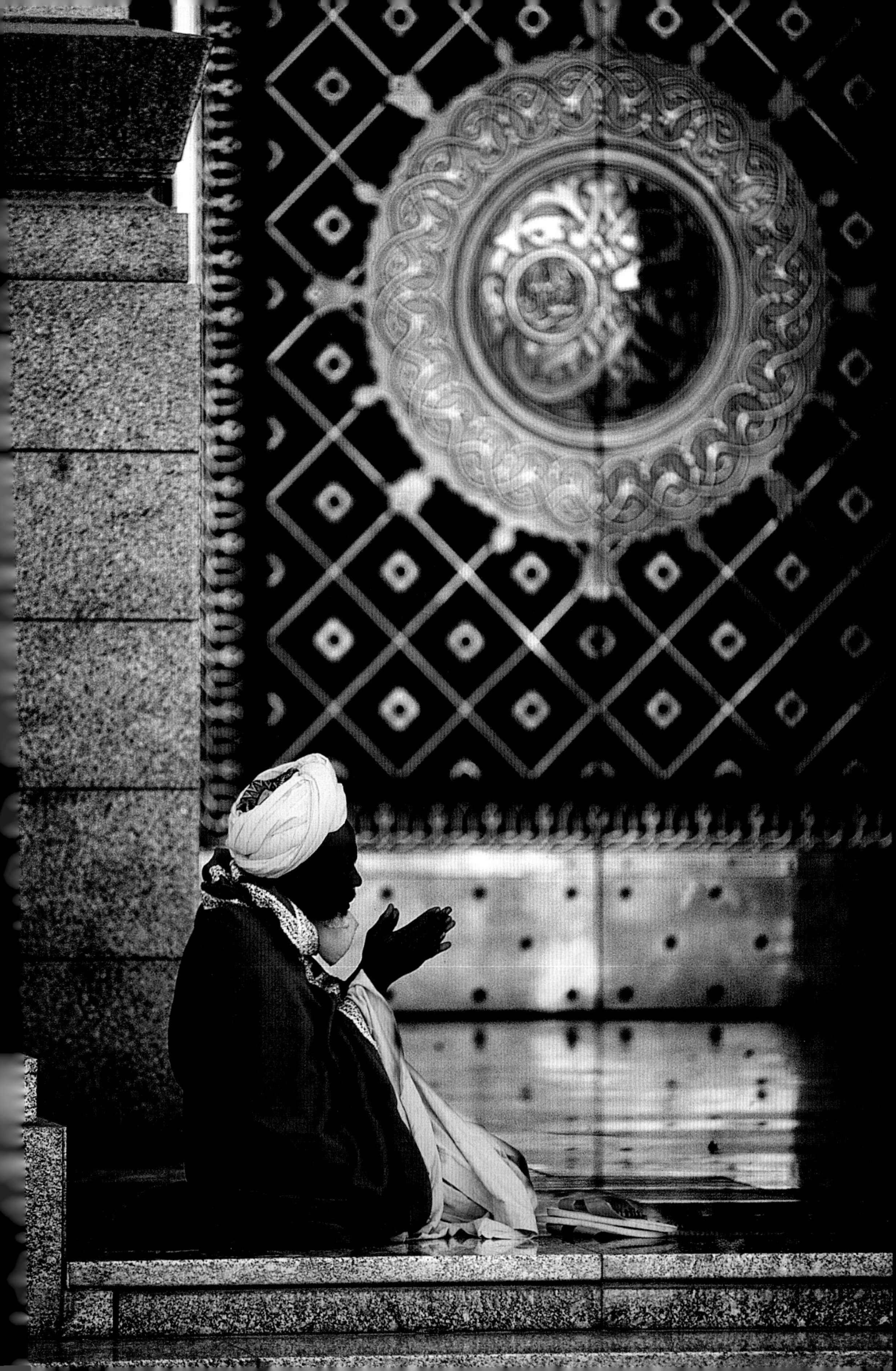

332-333 Children of foreign workers study at a Medina Quran school. Many residents of Mecca and Medina are descendants of people from all over the world who came on pilgrimages and, rather than return home, settled permanently.

334-335 Urged on by summonses from
mosque loudspeakers, worshippers hurry
along the marble courtyard to sunset prayers
at the Mosque of the Prophet.

336-337 Pilgrims enjoy *Iftar*, the evening meal that concludes the day-long fast every day during the month of Ramadan. The food for *Iftar* is donated by Medina philanthropists.

338-339 Pilgrims partaking of the *Iftar* meal on the grounds of the Mosque of the Prophet. Everyone who gets safely through a fast day offers a short prayer of gratitude before breaking fast.

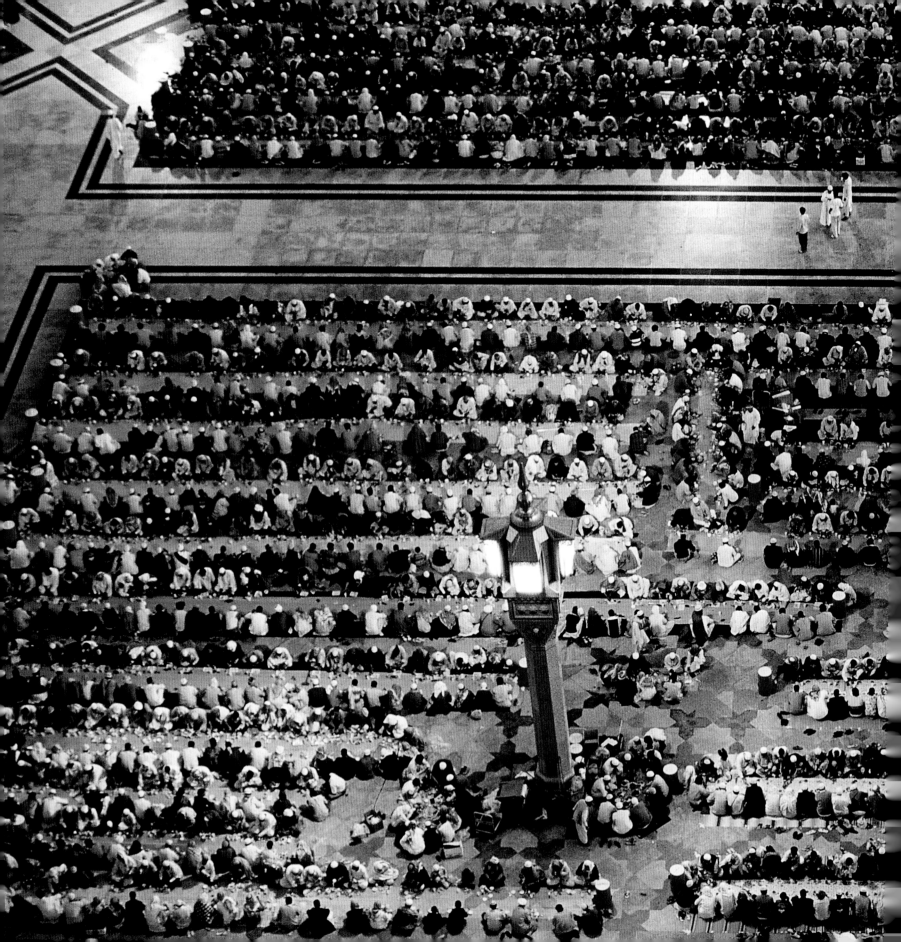

340-341 With one accord everyone – and not only at Medina – takes part in the Friday congregational prayer, prior to which the Imam delivers a 30-minute sermon.

342-343 In donning the *ihram*, the pilgrim prepares his or her heart for worship. Suitably attired, the pilgrim is ready for departure.

THE NILE

CIVILIZED RIVER,
PRIMITIVE RIVER

NUBIA

NILE FLOODING

•⌒

EOPLE ARE DRAWN TO PLACES FOR THE STRANGEST REASONS. THE FIRST INSPIRATION I EVER RECEIVED FROM THE NILE CAME TO ME ON THE BANK OF A LITTLE STREAM IN THE SAHARA.

The temperature was 50°C. It was August 1975; I'd been in the desert for a year and was flat broke. Having asked a friend to send money for gas to get me back to Europe, I waited, camping in the shade of coconut palms on the edge of an oasis where there was a post office. Would the money never arrive?

The stream was partly dried up, and here and there in its exposed bed were stagnant little pools, so salty you couldn't even wash in them. Idly contemplating the pools through the heat haze, I had my sudden flash of inspiration: "Nile!" The mighty Nile, flowing swiftly through this very Sahara, 13,200 miles (4000 km) south to north and never running dry!

The flooding of Nile begins in mid-June, when the Egyptian desert heat becomes hard to bear and Sirius is visible just before dawn in the eastern sky. Now as in the days of ancient Egypt, the river's bounty signifies rebirth. Every whiff of that putrid salt carried by the hot wind seemed to breed fresh visions of the Nile in my head as I waited, unable to move, a prisoner of the desert.

Five years were to pass before I began my Nile journey in October 1980 – an upstream journey from mouth to source.

After crossing Egypt in the Land Cruiser we brought from Europe, my assistant and I boarded a ferry in Aswan, Egypt's southernmost city. The ferry would take us across Lake Nasser into Sudan. Lake Nasser, 250 miles (400 km) from north to south, is an immensely long artificial lake, a byproduct of the Aswan Dam.

The boat was dreadful, drafted into ferry service for its vehicle-carrying capacity, such as it was – a crazy old tub, symbolizing to perfection the rigors of a journey into the African interior. It had no name and no cabins. Four cars had been loaded onto its 100-foot (30 m) steel deck. Roped to the left and right gunwales were two tattered boats with no engines – scraps of iron plate and plywood held together somehow. The ferry was terribly overcrowded, literally overflowing with passengers – Nubians returning from jobs in Egypt, loaded down with purchases and anticipating a triumphant homecoming. Lacking just about every instrument needed for navigation, the ferry put in to shore for the night, firing up the engines for departure at dawn. Not surprisingly, given the conveyance, a journey of less than 250 miles (400 km) took all of three days.

Along the way, the mountain of garbage got higher by the minute. Flies hovered, rats scurried. Passengers

submitted indifferently to having DDT sprayed over them. Nibbling on bread they had brought with them, scooping up lake water in empty cans and drinking it, they gave every impression of enjoying the trip. Watching them, I could not help but be deeply moved. This was Africa, I thought – the real Africa.

A sandy road connects Wadi Halfa on the Sudan side of Lake Nasser to Khartoum, the capital, 620 miles (1000 km) away. Nowhere in the entire Nile valley is the environment more demanding than in this northern Sudan region of Nubia. A few green oases scattered here and there along the riverbank are blessed with favorable topography and shaded by lush date palms; otherwise, most of the region is an uninhabited expanse of sand. In Egypt, dams have eliminated flooding; here, the ancient cycle of flood

and ebb persists to this day. In flood, the river overflows with dark gray water laden with earth and sand.

People's skin becomes gradually blacker as you proceed south. A particularly notable custom is the carving of tribal emblems into both cheeks. Men and women alike do this. Each tribe is different, but broadly speaking the emblems consist of three deep gashes, horizontal or vertical. The men's eyes glitter so fiercely, their facial expression is so peculiar, that they made me flinch at first, though once I got used to it I realized how kindly they are at heart – quite beyond comparison with Egyptians, who tend to take tourists for granted. Here, you drive past a house and the owner stops you, beckoning and calling: "Faattar, faattar," meaning "Come inside and rest, drink some tea......"

BLUE NILE

LIFE FLOWING THROUGH
THE DESERT

348-349 The Blue Nile flows from the
Ethiopian highlands into the Sudanese
desert. In a land of blistering heat and
sandstorms, the waters of the Nile are all
there is that keeps life going.

350-351 A man tries to entice a donkey onto a ferry sailboat near Dongola in northern Sudan. From Khartoum to Aswan in Egypt there is not a single bridge across the Nile.

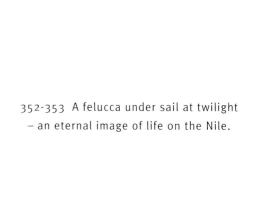

352-353 A felucca under sail at twilight
– an eternal image of life on the Nile.

354-355 An old woman pays her respects at a saint's tomb at a mosque in downtown Cairo. To elderly believers, mosques are places of repose and open-hearted meditation.

356 and 357 Farmers crossing the almost dry Atbara River, popularly known as the Black Nile.
Frequently in spate during the rainy season, its flow ebbs and almost ceases once the rains are past.

358-359 Near the confluence of the
Atbara and Nile Rivers, farmers head
home across the shallows. Egyptian
civilization was born of desert and water.

NUBA

SAVANNAH MOUNTAIN VILLAGE

T HE KORDOFAN SAVANNA OF SOUTH-
ERN SUDAN IS ROUGHLY THE SIZE OF HOKKAI-
DO, PUNCTUATED HERE AND THERE WITH THE
LOW MOUNTAINS OF THE NUBA MOUNTAIN
RANGE, THEIR TALLEST PEAKS LESS THAN
3300 FT (1000 M), THEIR EXPOSED GRANITE
MAKING FOR HARSH SCENERY.

The Nuba region is home to 500,000 people of
the Nuba tribe. A surprising fact about this tribe is
that it is divided into 50 subgroups, each speaking
a totally distinct language. A Nuban crossing a
mountain would be unable to communicate with
his fellow Nubans on the other side. Their customs
vary so widely that they claim their ancestors originally belonged to several tribes widely scattered
from the Nile bank to the savanna.

At some uncertain date in the past brutal slave
traders from the north began to infest the region.
Anthropologists and historians believe that the
Nuba of today are descended from ancestors of
diverse tribal origins who concealed themselves in
the mountains in order to escape the clutches of the
traders. Civilization was slow to penetrate these
isolated mountains. As recently as thirty years ago
clothing was completely unknown; people went
about their business stark naked. Ornamentation,
for both men and women, was a matter of slashing

the skin with knives so that the scars formed various decorative designs – a manner of adornment
inherited from the savage Africa of thousands of
years ago.

Veneration of the body is the heart of Nuban
aesthetics, whose celebration of masculine strength
finds its most characteristic expression in
wrestling. Wrestling matches dominate the harvest
festivities. My visit in November coincided with the
wrestling bouts at the end of the millet harvest.

Knowing none of the local languages, making
do with my smattering of Arabic, I spent six days
walking from village to village. Once I fell in with
a group of young people, their powerful bodies
painted with ash. Spears in hand, they were making their way across the withered fields. "El
Uheimah," they said, pointing toward a steep
rocky mountain in the distance. The sound of
drumming from the foot of Mount El Uheimah
echoed in the morning stillness. The wrestling
was about to begin.

The bouts are held on the stubble-clad millet
fields that have just been harvested. The wrestlers
cut brave, if strange, figures as they assembled,
their ash-smeared bodies clad in colorful pants and
strips of cloth, spears and old-fashioned guns
strapped to their backs. Attending them were

361 A young woman, her face decorated with artful scars.

young girls, their bodies coated all over with oil, their beautiful wild black skin gleaming in the fierce early afternoon sun. On their heads they carried vases filled with beer called Marise. This would go to the winners.

When the sun began its decline shortly after three o'clock, several men hoisting village flags ran onto the field to pour out the sacred ash. At this signal hundreds of men, wrestlers and villagers, surged forward like a vast wave, trampling the withered grass. A horn wailed; the men's shouts rose to a roar that pierced the clouds of dust they raised. At length

the massive, chaotic whirlpool settled, and the bouts began. A kind of rapture seemed to seize the wrestlers; their shouts and cries seemed hardly human. On the sidelines of the ferocious combat, the girls sang and danced. Winners were carried home in triumph on the shoulders of their supporters, the cheers of the girls ringing in their ears; the losers' supporters cried out in vexation and stamped their feet in frustration.

The champion is presented with an acacia twig. His back, anointed with consecrated ash, gleams golden in the setting sun.

362-363 Young girls playing in a village
clearing under a baobab tree. Baobab
fruit tastes like very sour syrup.

364 and 365 The entrance to a house's granary, designed to keep rats out, is high and so narrow that only children can penetrate it. When not in use it is covered with a lid.

366 and 367 Nuba women cooking. A family residence consists of four or five cylindrical buildings set around a courtyard.

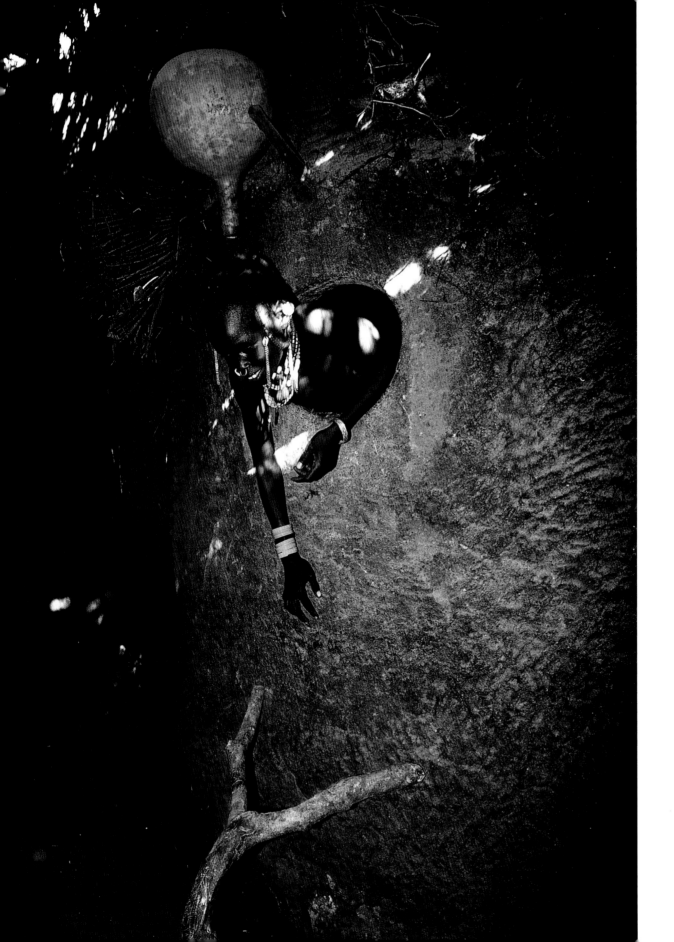

368-369 and 369 Nuba girls gather at a wrestling meet to cheer on their champions. The girls' skin, decorated with beads and cowrie shells, is oiled to a splendid black glow. Girls who cheered for winning wrestlers shout for joy and carry the victors home in triumph. Those who supported losers groan and stamp their feet in chagrin.

371 Nuban wrestling matches, part of the harvest festival, are held around December, after
the harvest has been brought in. Nubans regard masculine strength as the highest virtue.

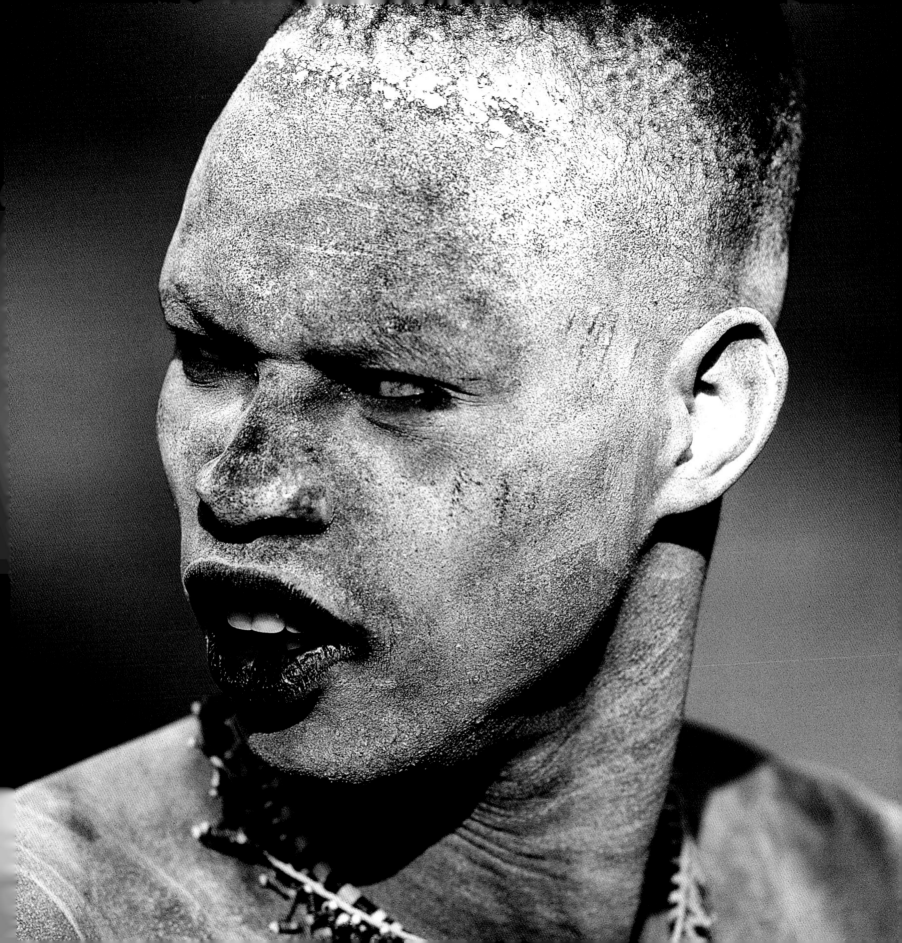

373 The consecrated ashes with which wrestlers coat their bodies are produced
by burning acacia twigs. Winners are coated afresh in "victory ashes."

374-375 Before the matches,
wrestlers feast on cakes of ground
millet and okra soup.

376 Nuba wrestling is confined to standing techniques. A wrestler wins by knocking his opponent down. The winner then goes on to meet the next challenger.

377 The winner is carried home on the shoulders of his supporters and decked in victory ashes.

378 and 378-379 Dances in praise of the winning
wrestler. The dances are long and the rhythm is
fierce. The best dancers among the girls are
rewarded with money slipped into their bodices.

DINKA & NUER

THE SYMBIOTIC LIVES OF MEN AND THEIR CATTLE

F OUR HOURS BY CESSNA SOUTH OF KHARTOUM LIES THE GREAT MARSH KNOWN AS SUDD. THE WHITE NILE, MEANDERING NORTH THROUGH THE SAVANNA, MERGES HERE INTO THE BOG, ITS SURFACE COVERED BY PAPYRUS REEDS.

"Sudd," in Arabic, suggests barriers, closed-in spaces. Enveloped in heat and humidity, the Sudd is home to countless floating islands formed by water plants and papyrus reeds drift-ing downstream and accumulating in the marsh. Shifting with the currents and the wind, the islands break up and reform endlessly.

During the rainy season, the flooding of the Nile and the especially heavy rains of the Sudd submerge the lowlands, enlarging the marsh to an expanse the size of Japan – 148,875 sq. mi. (377,815 sq. km). The rainy season lasts half the year, making overland passage difficult. No won-der civilization was slow to penetrate. To this day it is considered one of the world's last unex-plored regions. Richard Burton and John Speke and then Samuel Baker were among the noted 19th-century explorers who boldly ventured as far upstream as the Sudd in search of the Nile's source found their further advance – and their retreat as well – blocked by the floating islands;

many of them starved or succumbed to local dis-eases.

We flew on and on, seeing nothing below but a chaos of water and vegetation. Suddenly a lone canoe appeared. Two men, one in front, one behind. Their oars rippled the gray water. We circled overhead, flying low to get a better look. The men stopped paddling and looked up. They were stark naked. Still circling, we descended further. One of the men brandished his oar as if it were a spear. Evidently he found this strange mechanical bird threatening.

The men were Sudd fishermen of the Dinka tribe. Later we visited one of their settlements. The thatch-roofed huts by the water's edge rest-ed on 20-inch (50-cm) high earthen mounds. The elevation kept them dry in the rainy season and when the river flooded. Using simple nets, the men fished day after day, catching no more than the settlement needed for food. One of them was missing part of a thigh. A crocodile ate it, he said.

One day the men announced they were going hippopotamus-hunting; would I care to join them? The men, harpoons in hand, set out in two canoes. We made our way to a floating island some 3300 feet (1000 m) in diameter. Walking on

381 A Dinka cattle camp at dusk. Smoke from burning cow dung keeps the mosquitoes at bay.

it was hazardous – press your foot down too solidly and you end up in the water. "No noise," said the men, and I walked more gingerly than ever. In the middle of the island, parting the grass, the hunters made a breathing hole for the hippo and then, to drive it there, set fires around the island's edges. The men then gathered round the hole, harpoons at the ready. For two hours we waited, scarcely daring to breathe. I had my camera ready, imagining horrific scenes of blood and frenzy. But the hippo never appeared. Exhausted, we returned to the canoes. The evening sky was blazing red. The Nile – what a primitive turn this river of civilization takes, I thought, as it flows through Sudan!

Traveling overland, I had arrived in the Sudd in April, just as the dry season was ending. The savanna grass had withered and yellowed. Here and there the locals were setting fire to the old grass, the better to nurture the new pasturage that would spring up in the rains soon to come. As night fell on the blazing fires, the sound of drumming arose from the nearby livestock camps – pulsing, throbbing rhythms; backdrop, it seemed to me, of some wild African opera, and I watched, totally absorbed, far into the night.

Two Sudd tribes, the Nuer and the Dinka, live off their herds – live, indeed, in such close proximity to their beasts that anthropologists consider them a unique subject of research.

In the rainy season, when the flooding White Nile turns the lowlands into swamp, the tribes retreat to their villages on high ground, but as the dry season advances they camp in the low-lying pasture land by the water's edge. Here man and beast live as one. In the Sudd, where malaria is always a threat, the tribespeople have devised an effective protection against the disease-bearing mosquito. They burn cow dung through the night. The smoke, they say, is prime insect-repellent.

My purpose in coming to the Sudd was to live in a herdsmen's camp and share their lives as I photographed them. How to do that, though, not knowing a word of their language? Should I hire a guide? No, better do what I always did – go by myself and play it by ear. That's how I worked throughout my coverage of the Nile, and most of the time things went smoothly enough. I believe I can truly say that in the course of many years spent traveling in remote places at the risk of my life, I have acquired a persona that puts the people I meet at ease. I've never had any trouble on my own. Only when I've tried to use townspeople as intermediaries have problems arisen. As for the language barrier, what did it matter? I wasn't there to research a thesis. Our small store of Arabic would do for getting our basic feelings across to one another.

What surprised me most as I established myself in camp was the complete lack of any fence, hedge or other partition between the men and their animals. To the extent that such a partition signifies civilization, then what I witnessed there was a kind of precivilized honeymoon period in the long history of coexistence between humans and animals. The men slept with their herds on cow dung ash among mounds of smoldering cow droppings whose smoke kept the mosquitoes away. They awoke each morning to the sound of lowing cattle. The older men, incidentally, remained in the nearby village. The men camping with the herds were mostly young. As soon as the animals began to pass water the men hurried to them to wash their faces in the streaming urine. Then they milked the cows, rubbing their horns as a sign of affection, smearing ash on their backs, removing the bugs from them – eager, in short, to do whatever they could for them. Such was their way, unchanged no doubt for thousands of years; men and livestock living together in happy symbiosis.

Herders, according to one anthropologist's report, conferred their own given names on their favorite cows. They dedicated songs of praise to them. Their love for their cows resembles the blind love of a doting parent for a favorite child. They divide cattle into at least twenty-seven distinct categories according to coat color and color distribution. I had a scientific book about cattle with me, and when I showed them the illustrations, even the children, with great excitement, accurately called out the name of each one. No wonder. They live with cows from infancy. When they are hungry they milk a cow and drink their fill; they groom themselves by smearing their bodies with cow dung ash; they sleep on mattresses made from cow hides.

When at last they drive the cows out to pasture, the herdsmen collect the dung that fell overnight and divide it into small mounds, spreading them out to dry. In the evening they heap up the dried dung and burn it. When the cows return to camp, the men hoist their flags and sing songs to celebrate their beasts, trotting with them one lap around the camp. The cattle, for their part, would be unable to survive on the savanna, where enemies abound, without painstaking human care.

In the morning cool before sunrise, contemplating the men and beasts and the life they so intimately shared, I recalled a wall painting I had seen deep in the Sahara. It depicted the same man-cow symbiosis I was seeing here. It was some 6000 years old.

Two years after my visit to southern Sudan, the nation's Islamic government abruptly proclaimed its intention to place the entire country under shariya, Islamic law. Most of the south is either Christian or animist. The imposition on non-Muslims of shariya – which among other things bans alcohol – is a gross violation of their human rights. As state policy it is absurd.

A simmering North-South antipathy consequently flared into all-out civil war. For the south, ravaged by massacre and starvation, it was devastating. The life I glimpsed there in 1981, man and beast living in symbiotic harmony, seems to have been traditional African culture's last gasp.

384-385   The White Nile winding its way
through the great marsh known as the
Sudd. 160 km downstream from Juba in
southern Sudan, the White Nile flows
into a vast marsh crowded with islands
of floating tufts of thick grass.

386-387 A canoe threading its way among the floating islands. Nile perch and other fish caught by fishermen with nets form the main part of the local diet.

388 A youth walks homeward carrying the head of a gazelle caught by a domestic
dog. Countless wild beasts inhabit the savanna surrounding the camp.

390-391 A Dinka tribesman collects fresh-fallen cow dung. Piles of burning cow dung smoulder all through the night. The Sudd, infested with malaria-bearing mosquitoes, would be uninhabitable without the cow dung smoke that keeps them off.

392-393 Men carrying away an animal that has died of disease. Livestock are never killed, except as sacrifices, so a beast that dies of disease is a precious food resource. When a valued cow is lost, "Our eyes and heart are sad, but our teeth and bellies are glad," as a local expression has it.

394-395 The camp awakes to the sound of the lowing of the cattle. Soon after the milking is done, the men drive the stock to pasture.

396-397 A Dinka man knitting one of the ropes
that restrain the livestock during the night. The
men sleep on the ashes of burnt cattle dung
within a circle of withered trees.

398 Breathing into a cow's uterus provides a sexual stimulation under which the cow produces more milk. With his right hand the boy lightly strokes the cow's udder.

399 A boy washes his hair in cow urine. Children raised in such close proximity to cattle feel no disgust towards animal urine or dung.

400-401 A boy of the Nuer tribe sucks on a cow's udder. After stimulating milk production by breathing into the cow's uterus, the young people drink its milk. It is their only breakfast.

402 and 403 A man assiduously attends to another's hair. Thoroughly rubbing ashes into the hair drives away fleas and lice. Men coat their entire bodies with ashes.

404-405 After wetting the hair with cow urine, the
curls are carefully arranged with the aid of a splinter
of acacia wood. The gold color is the result of
ammonium in the urine.

405 A Dinka tribesman "made up" with cow dung ash.

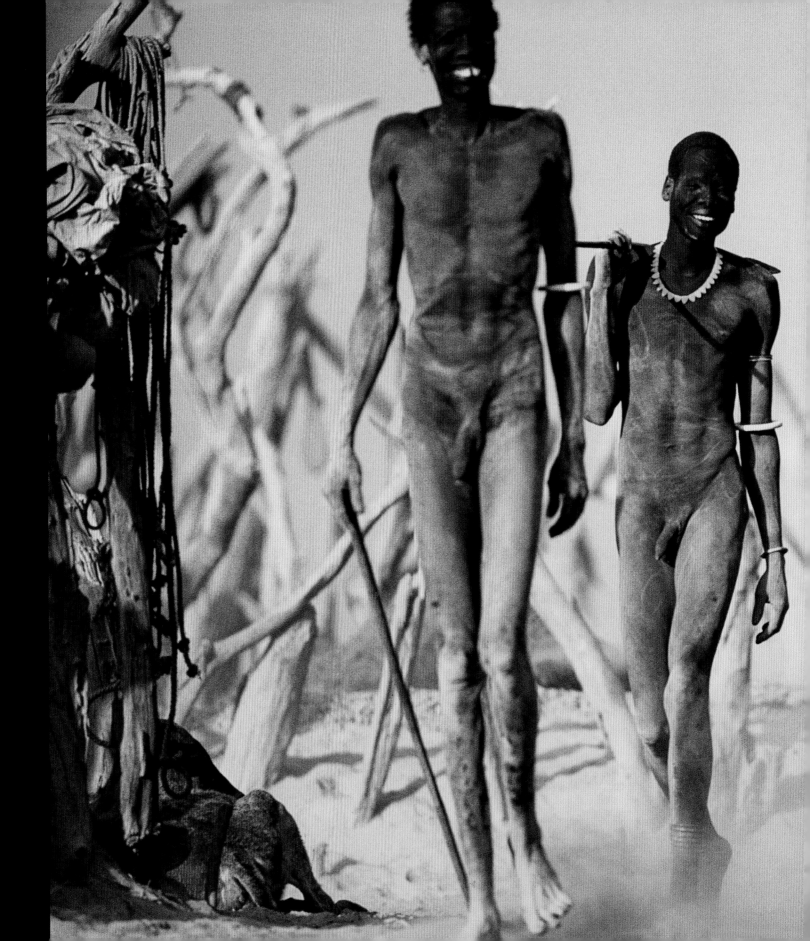

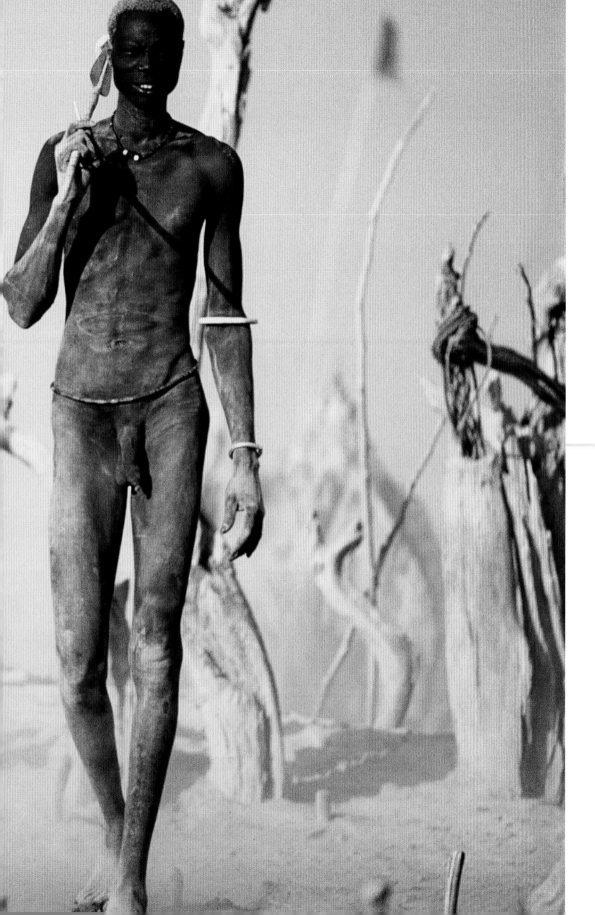

406-407 Dinka men, tall and slim, wear round ivory bracelets on their left arms. Here they return from the pasture.

408-409 A Dinka youth has his body
coated with ashes. Once the livestock
has been driven out to pasture, the men
in camp are much preoccupied with the
care of their bodies.

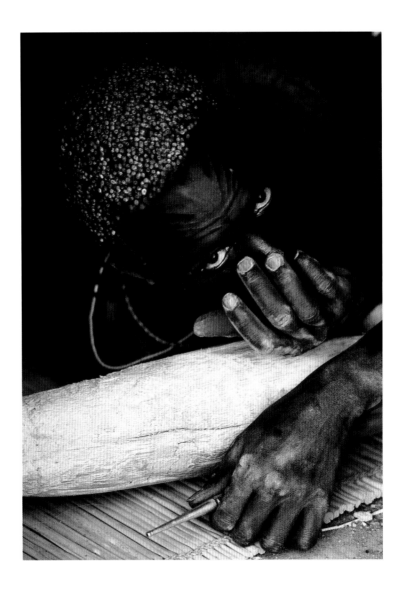

410-411 Men escape the intense outdoor heat by taking their rest
in a hut. Most of the men living in camp are young. Old people
and women live in the village on high ground.

411 The triple "V" carved on this man's forehead is the symbol of
the Dinka tribe.

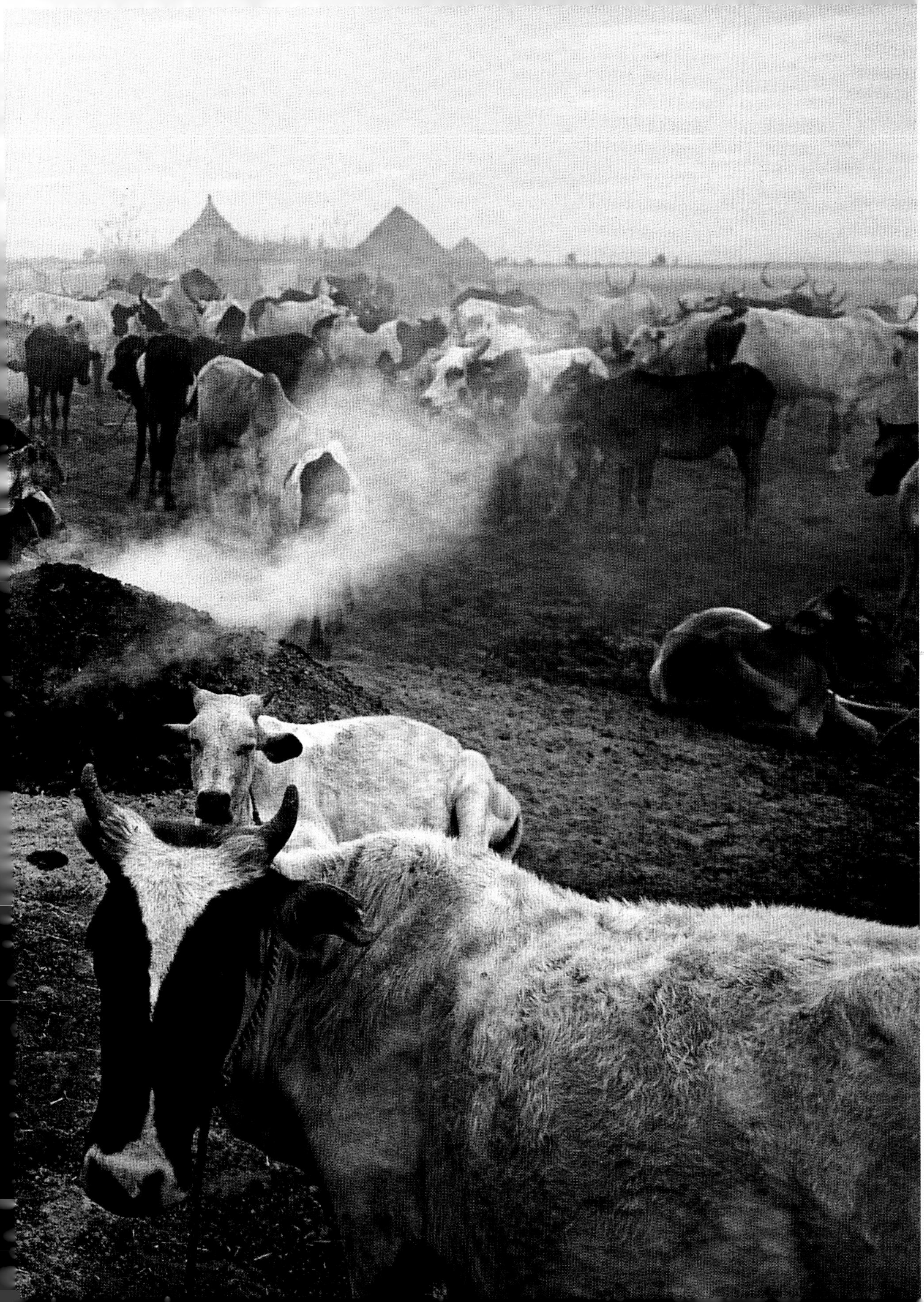

412-413 Nuer tribespeople, long known for their warlike ways, frequently attack Dinka camps in order to steal their cattle.

414-415 This camp near the White Nile, owing to rising water levels in the river, becomes a bog once the rainy season sets in, and people move back to the village on high ground.

416-417 A Nuer girl preparing the evening meal. Milk products and millet are the diet staples.

418-419 A dance in honor of the livestock. Outisde the circle of the dance an intrepid bull is led around.

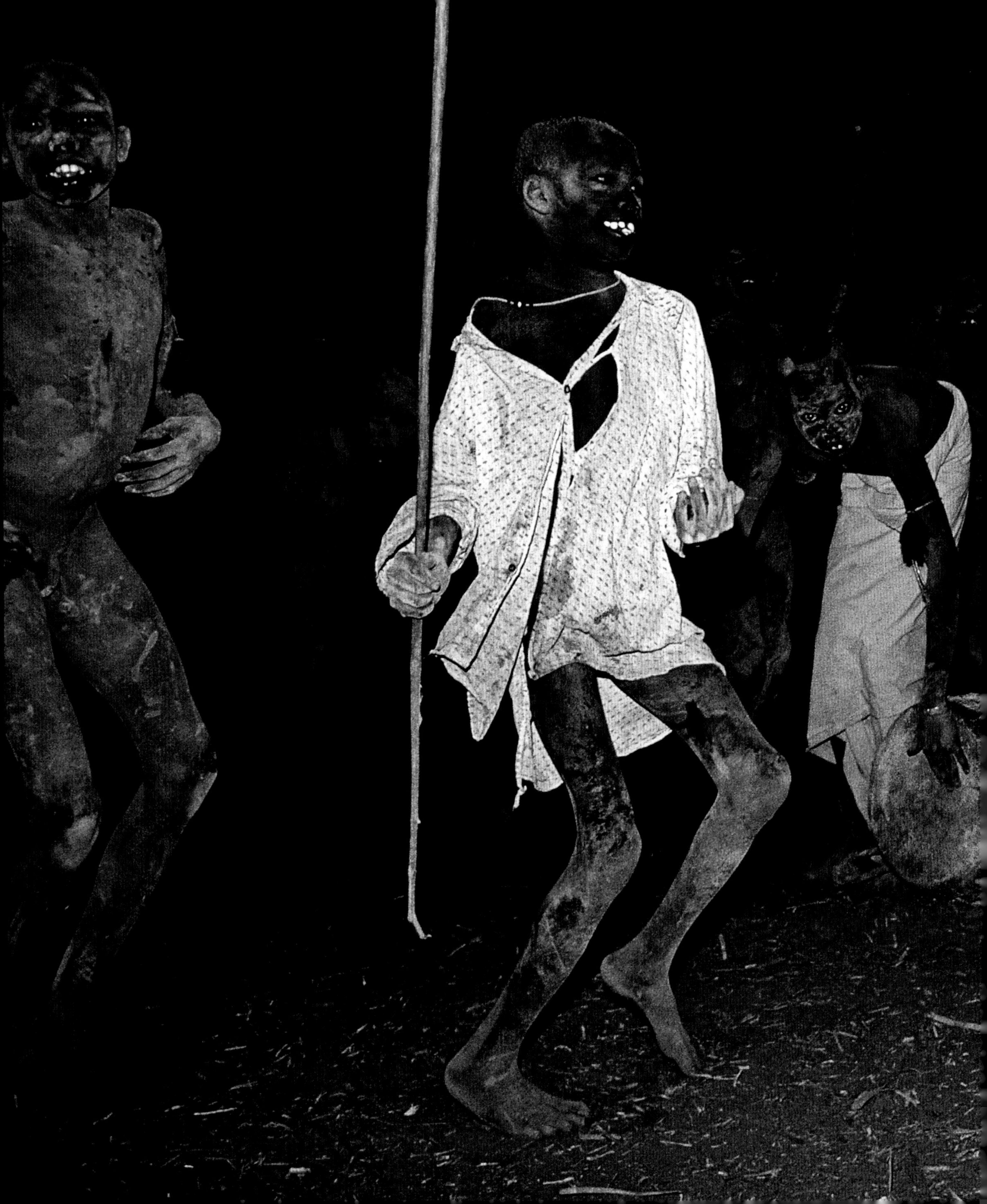

THE GREAT RIFT VALLEY

CRADLE OF THE HUMAN RACE

THE GREAT RIFT VALLEY

CRADLE OF THE HUMAN RACE

T HE GREAT RIFT VALLEY IS AN IMMENSE-LY LONG CRACK IN THE EARTH'S SURFACE, SNAKING ITS WAY THROUGH 248 MILES (4000 KM) OF EAST AFRICA FROM MOZAMBIQUE TO ETHIOPIA, THEN EXTENDING NORTHWARD BEYOND THE AFRICAN CONTINENT, FROM THE RED SEA THROUGH ISRAEL'S DEAD SEA AND ON INTO TURKEY – 4340 MILES (7000 KM) FROM END TO END.

Originally formed by powerful movements of the earth's crust, the rift is widening even now at the rate of several centimeters a year. Eventually – some 40 million years from now – it will be a sea similar in shape to the Red Sea. It will cut the African continent in two.

The subterranean pressures that created the Great Rift Valley also threw up land elevations on both sides of it, elongated plateaus whose inner strata are prone to major cave-ins, which in turn have helped shape the valley. The plateaus, 4950 – 8250 ft (1500-2500 m) above sea level, are generally favored with pleasant climates, while the valley itself, 3300 ft (1000 m) lower down, swelters in relentless heat. Almost all the lakes in the valley are extremely salty, and in two of them, Lakes Magadi and Natron near the Kenya-Tanzania border, the soda content supports algae whose characteristic red coloring seems to turn the lakes into seas of blood.

The Great Rift Valley is a harsh landscape of volcanoes, lava flows, fissures, deserts and salt flats – and yet this forbidding environment nurtured the human species in its infancy. Mountains on its western rim prevented the prevailing westerly winds from penetrating the valley. The consequent dessication turned forest into savanna; the apes whose habitat it was, says the most widely accepted theory, were compelled to adapt by learning to walk on two feet. It was a first step on the long road to human evolution. West of the mountains, where the westerlies blew unobstructed and the lush forest remained intact, evolution favored the anthropoid apes – gorillas, chimpanzees, bonobos and so on. The theory does not go unchallenged, but it is a matter of fact that the fossils of primitive humans excavated in the Great Rift Valley reflect the course of four million years of evolution, and there can be no doubt that this elongated crevice deserves its designation as "cradle of the human race."

Today nomad cattle herders inhabit the region. A relentless struggle for existence – against hunger, against equally hard-pressed neighboring tribes – has left its mark on their features, which are fierce. Their wildness is in stark contrast to the mild-mannered farmers of the plateaus. Fascinated alike by the extraordinary landscape and the desperate way of life it has bred, I have returned to this wasteland again and again.

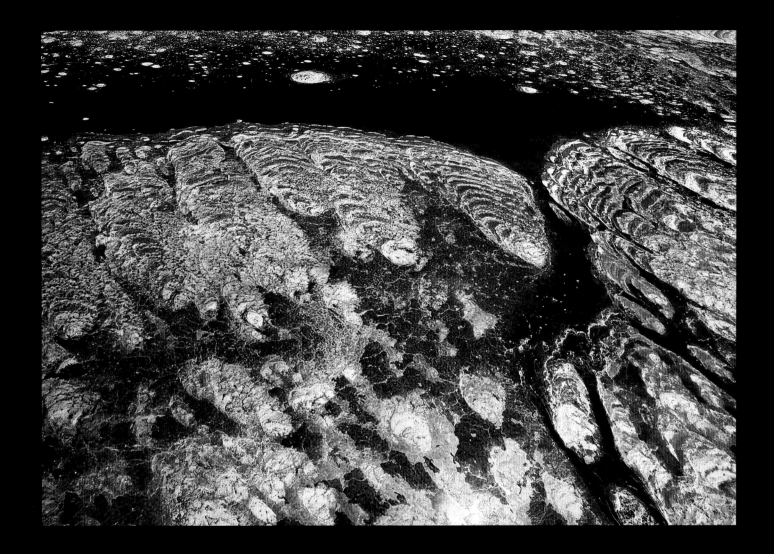

420 A girl of the Galeb tribe of the Omo Valley carries water in a gourd.

423 Lake Natron in northern Tanzania. The lake surface bears an uncanny resemblance to flowing blood.

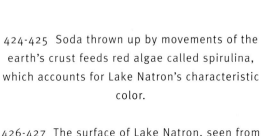

424-425 Soda thrown up by movements of the
earth's crust feeds red algae called spirulina,
which accounts for Lake Natron's characteristic
color.

426-427 The surface of Lake Natron, seen from
a helicopter that has descended to an altitude
of 30 meters. As the dry season advances,
rapid evaporation causes the soda to
crystallize. Soda crystals form plank-like
coverings over the lake surface.

428-429 Next to Lake Natron is Lake Magadi in
Kenya. Magadi is another soda lake. The plank-
like crystal formation at left grows to a
thickness of one meter during the dryest part
of the year – one could drive a car over it.

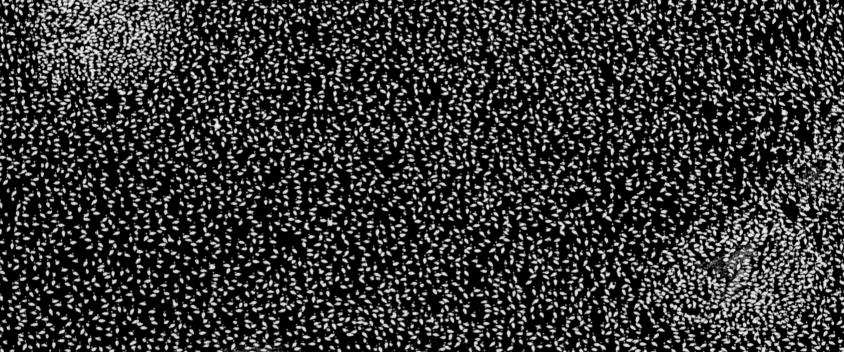
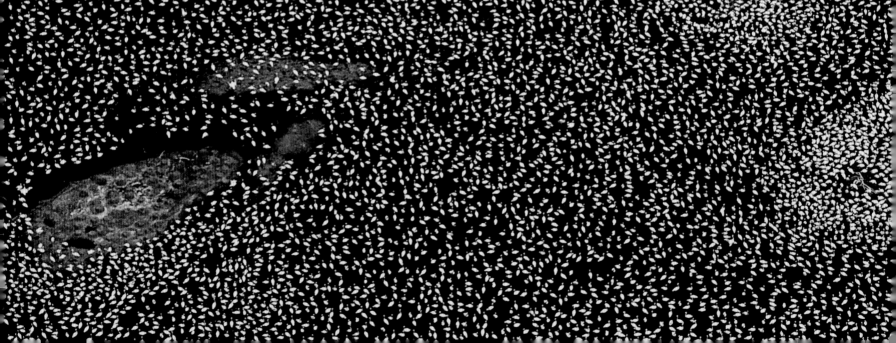

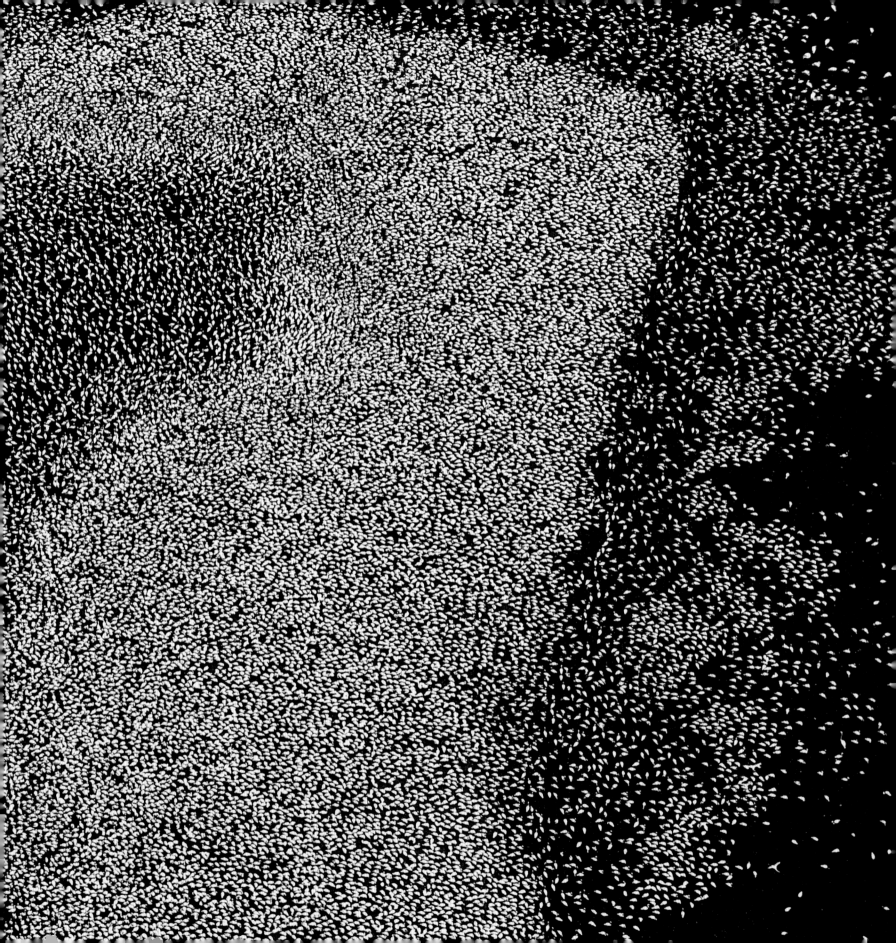

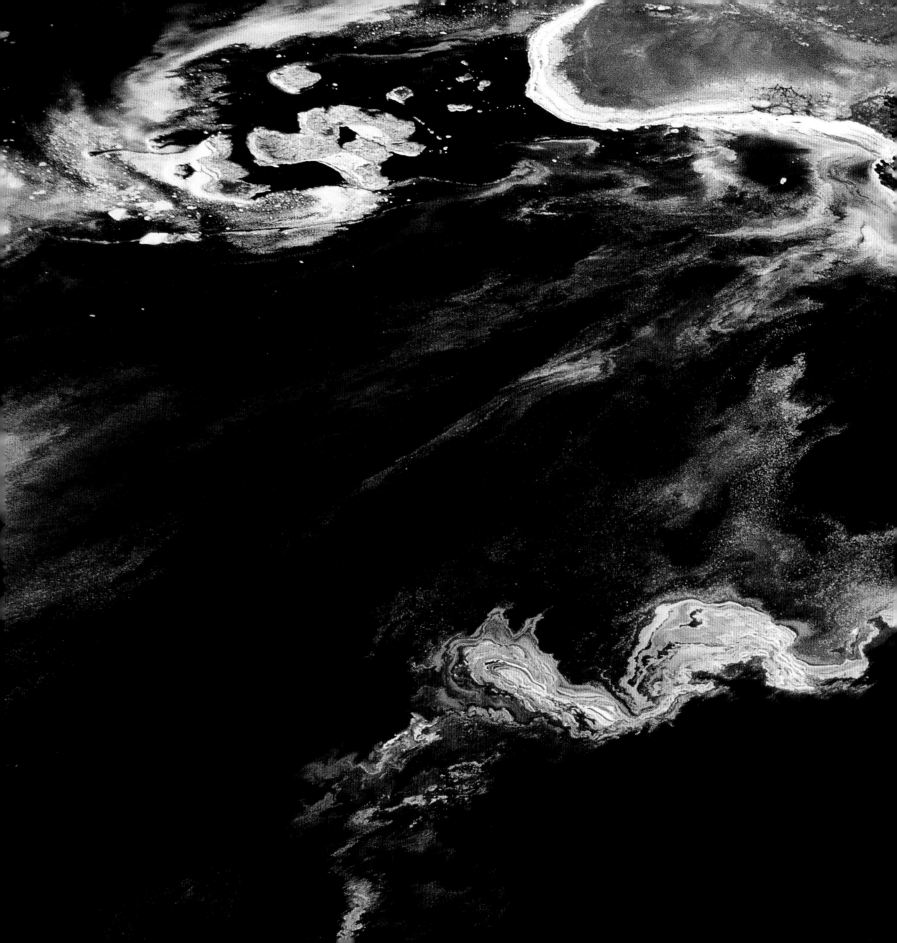

430-431 Flamingoes, their wings stained pink
by the algae they feed on, jostle for space on
Lake Bogoria in central Kenya.

432-433 Soda crystals flowing with the wind
form stripe patterns on the surface of the lake.
When the rainy season comes the crystals
dissolve in the influx of water, and the lake
presents a view more or less like any other lake.

434-435 Africa's highest peak at 19,453 ft
(5895 m), Kilimanjaro is revered by the Masai
tribespeople as the mountain of the gods.
The glacier at its peak is receding, however –
an apparent casualty of global warming.

DANAKIL DESERT

TORRID SALT FLATS

IN THE DANAKIL DESERT EXTENDING FROM ETHIOPIA INTO DJIBOUTI LIVES THE AFAR OR DANAKIL TRIBE.

They are nicknamed "kin hunters" for their custom of severing the phalluses *(kin)* of their slain enemies and presenting them to their sweethearts. The presentation is understood as a marriage proposal.

The Danakil Desert is known for its extreme heat. With summer temperatures in some places rising to 50°C, it is considered the most inclement desert in the world. Ethiopians living in the cool plateaus 8250 ft (2500 m) above sea level recoil at the very mention of the Afar's name. A barbarous environment – heat, lava, craters, salt flats – has produced, they say, a barbarous people. In this blighted land, where hunger is as persistent as endemic disease, the Afar drive their herds of camels and goats, clashing over grazing land with the Issa tribe of neighboring Somalia. When Afar and Issa tribesmen set out to pasture their beasts, they carry automatic pistols for self-defense.

Midway between the Danakil Desert and the plateau is a town called Bati, known for the large weekly Monday market that draws people from all the local tribes. On a hillock in the middle of the throng stands an odd-looking arch made of steel pipe. On the arch are two contraptions that look like pulleys for scooping up well water. But there is no well here, and the arch turns out to be a gallows – no longer in use, apparently, except perhaps as a dramatic symbol of law in an otherwise lawless land overrun with firearms.

I once had a brush of my own with the true nature of the Afar. It was terrifying. We were heading down from the plateau, my guide and I, when we saw a group of nomads and their livestock at a well in the valley 160 ft or so (ca. 50 m) below. We pulled over. Getting out of the car, I trained my telescopic lens on the scene. In the viewfinder I saw a man, Kalashnikov in hand . . . could that be me he was aiming at? With a strangled cry the guide pulled me down, hustled me into the car and drove off. The man must have taken my telescopic lens for a gun.

There are all kinds of rumors circulating about the Afar. I've spent time with them in their camps. It was tense at first, but once they accept a man, there's nothing to worry about. I felt no hostility toward me. As a foreigner, an outsider, I was of no particular interest to them. The children are brave livestock herders. Their good humor can turn abruptly ominous. The women, though Muslims, strut about with their breasts bared. Their brown skin is dazzling.

I asked the elders about "kin-hunting."

"We don't do that any more," they said. "But yes, it is part of our culture" – the culture of a hostile environment where enemies press hard upon one another. One phallus, they explained, was worth 100 camels.

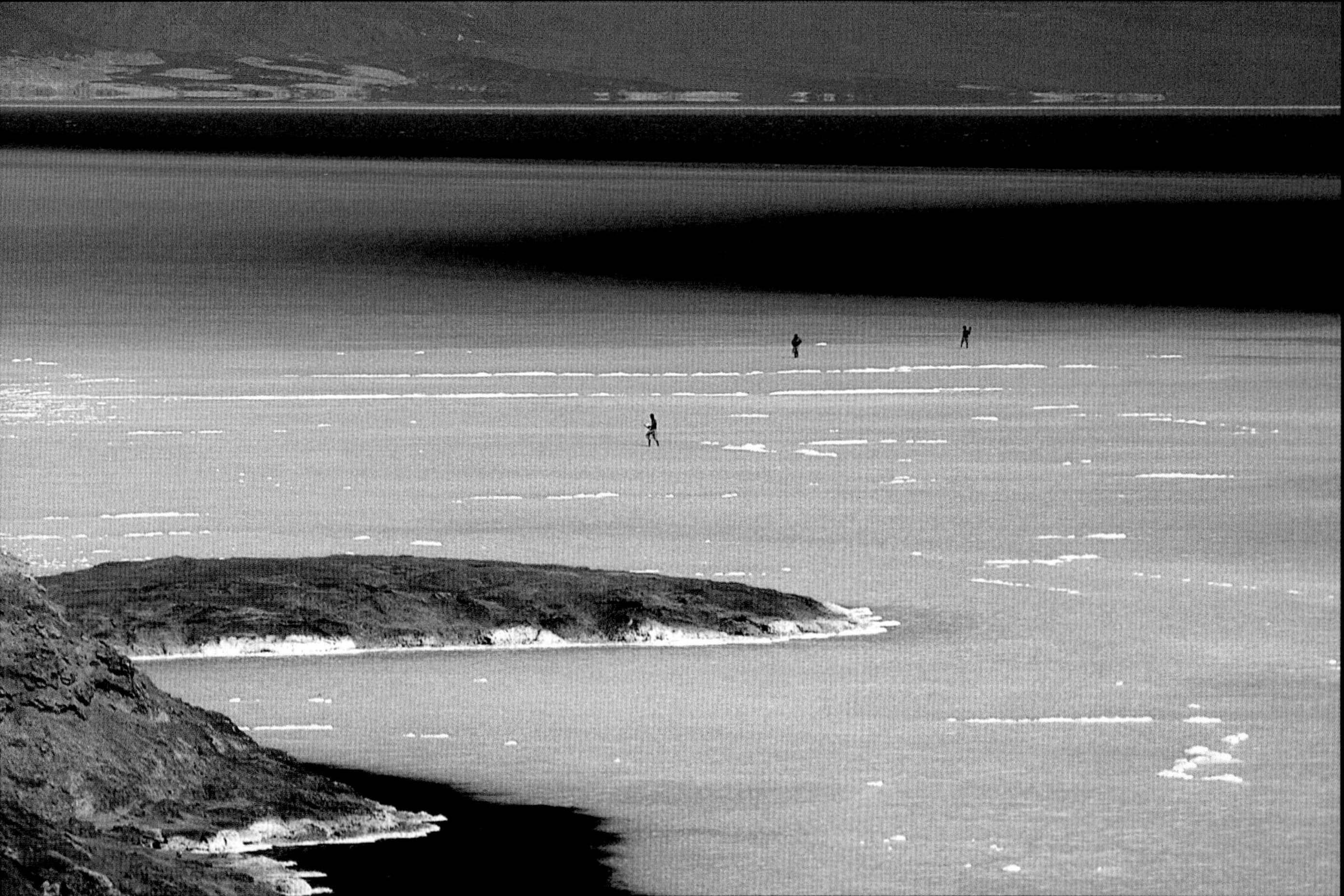

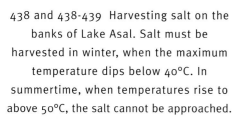

438 and 438-439 Harvesting salt on the banks of Lake Asal. Salt must be harvested in winter, when the maximum temperature dips below 40°C. In summertime, when temperatures rise to above 50°C, the salt cannot be approached.

440-441 This salt flat on the bank of Lake Assal is 6 miles (10 km) long and several km wide. Salt flats form when sea water penetrates cracks in the earth's crust and evaporates.

442-443 To avoid the heat, the caravans arrive at evening and the men dig for salt through the night, setting out the next morning.

444-445 The heat having at last abated,
nomads of the Danakil tribe perform
evening prayers outside their hut as the
livestock, raising clouds of dust, return
along the sand.

446-447 This wood-frame hut spread with straw matting provides barely enough space for the family to sleep. From the ceiling hang containers made of kid skin.

OMO VALLEY

THE LAST AFRICA

S OUTHWESTERN ETHIOPIA IS RICHLY WATERED BY THE OMO RIVER AS IT FLOWS FROM ITS SOURCE IN THE PLATEAU INTO LAKE TURKANA IN KENYA.

Many different tribes, stock farmers by occupation, live on the broad savanna downstream. Strange customs persist among them. There are tribes that have yet to discover clothing; some tribeswomen adorn their lips with large plates. There are no roads worthy of the name, and outsiders are rarely seen. The national government's writ scarcely runs here. "The last Africa," the region could be called – a world cut off from civilized society.

The revolution that overthrew Emperor Haile Selassie in 1974 installed in his stead a grim socialist military dictatorship. The borders closed as war with Somalia and a domestic guerrilla insurgency intensified. For seventeen years, until the dictatorship crumbled in 1991, foreign visitors required official permission to travel beyond the vicinity of Adis Abeba, the capital. A world travel boom beginning in the 1980s set in motion a fresh conquest of Africa, this one spearheaded by tour groups penetrating some of the continent's most inaccessible corners. The Omo River Valley, though, continued to be inaccessible to all but the most adventurous tourists. Few in number, their impact was minimal, and the area remained pristine. My first trip to the Omo region was in 1982. In the

nature park, unlike in Kenya, I saw no wild animals at all. They must have been there, but poaching by local tribespeople had taught them not to approach humans. Lawlessness was said to be pervasive. The government exercised no effective control, and tourists stayed away. Cut off from outsiders, the locals held fast to their own culture. The women wore garments of elaborately decorated goatskin; the frayed T-shirts and short pants one saw everywhere in Africa had yet to penetrate here. The main village held a weekly market which drew hundreds of people, all dressed in traditional garb, their hair plastered with pigment made of clay and butter. It made a grand and thrilling spectacle. The men wound short cloths round their waists, leaving their genitals exposed.

In 1991 the dictatorship collapsed, the civil war ended, and tourists began to inundate Ethiopia. Once the land borders opened, European tour groups poured into the Omo region from neighboring Kenya, eager to photograph of "the last Africa." Though still on a very small scale compared to other parts of Africa, the tourist influx was sufficient to alter local ways. My last visit to the Omo Valley was in 1997; I would point my camera and everyone, adults and children alike, would converge on me with outstretched hands: "Birr, birr, birr." The birr is a unit of Ethiopian currency, 1 birr being worth 0.1 euro. They had never had cash before; now it was

449 Women of the Hamar tribe, clothed in garments of cattle fur and adorned with bracelets and
necklaces of shells and metal. The Omo Valley is the last repository of traditional African customs

to be had for the asking from anyone wanting to photograph them. If you don't pay, the atmosphere can turn nasty. "The last Africa" has been turned on its ear.

At least ten principal tribes inhabit the Omo Valley – the Hamar, Galeb, Bodi, Surma, Mursi, Arbore and so on. Their numbers vary, from several hundred to 20-30,000. They live in perpetual, often violent conflict. Fiercely proud of their own tribes, they go to great lengths to emphasize any feature – clothing, hairstyle, women's cosmetics – that sets them apart from the others. Their love of their own is matched by a seething hatred toward hostile tribes. Bloody feuds sparked by cattle rustling can drag on for generations.

Professor Katsuyoshi Fukui of Kyoto University has studied the Bodi tribe for forty years. Once while he was staying with them, Bodi tribesmen raided a nearby agricultural settlement, killing hundreds and making off with more than 1000 head of cattle. The following year they attacked a different settlement, killing over 100. Only two Bodi died in the raids. The nomads are organized by age, fostering powerful ties among people in the same age-group. In a fight, each age-group, several individuals strong, mans a specific post. It makes for a potent and effective fighting force. Elders, wise with the wisdom of experience, devise the strategies. Assaults always begin at dawn.

The nomads' bellicosity is breathtaking. For example, when a valued cow dies, the bereaved owner vents his grief by venturing into enemy territory and killing one member of a hostile tribe. This is accepted practice, and the business is gone about quite casually. The easy accessibility, in recent years,

of high-performance firearms has oiled the flames of this belligerency. Africa's endless civil wars have flooded the continent with weapons. In the Omo Valley the going price of a gun is six head of cattle. The more or less ritualized tribal rivalries that once played out with arrows and spears are now gun-battles. The more guns there are, the more imperative grows the demand for still more. And so this society has fallen into a perverted situation: tribesmen who can manage very well without pants would not dream of venturing abroad without a gun.

As recently as 1995 – two years before my last visit to the region in 1997 – the Arbore and the Borana, eternal enemies, fought each other, with a death toll of four hundred. Police intervention was ineffectual, the combattants so surpassing them in terms of arms and fighting spirit that the policemen couldn't even get close.

Early one afternoon under a scorching sky in a village of the Karo tribe beside the Omo River, the men, guns and pillows in hand, gathered in the shade of trees to talk. The pillows, made from specially treated acacia wood, are designed to protect the characteristic tribal mud-hardened hair-dos during the customary afternoon nap. Wherever the men go they take their guns and their pillows.

On this particular afternoon, it was evident from the fiery tones of the men and the way they brandished their weapons as they spoke that they were recounting their heroic exploits. Stretched out on the ground nearby and watching them, I had the uncanny feeling of having fallen through a time warp into some totally alien dimension.

452-453 A Konso village, one of seven, laid out
at the top of a small mountain. The houses are
closely packed together – this village alone has
3000 residents – and arranged in a pattern
resembling contour lines on a map.

454-455 A youth transforms himself
into a fierce cheetah for a festival.

456 and 456-457 To create a face like this takes a full hour. The white and brown pigments are made from clay, the black from soot. To these cattle-raising people, carnivorous wild animals are their menacing natural enemies.

458 and 459 The hairstyle is hardened by clay, and ornaments made from ostrich feathers and various other things are thrust in at the top of the head and forehead. Since the arrangement comes apart as the hair grows, it must be created again from scratch.

459

460-461 People deep in the African interior can live quite comfortably without pants but not, they say, without guns. A Kalashnikov can be had in exchange for six cows.

462 and 462-463 Girls of the Hamar tribe,
their faces decorated with clay makeup and
their hair stiffened with earth and butter, wait
for the dance to begin.

464-465 and 465 A Hamar tribal dance in honor of a youth's Jumping of the Bull ceremony. The boy approaches the girls by repeatedly jumping in their direction. Hip against hip, they make gestures suggestive of sexual intercourse, then separate.

466-467 Women sing, rubbing
their bracelets together and
keeping the rhythm. The elliptical
metal fragments on their heads
symbolize ostrich beaks.

468-469 The jumping and leaping go on and on, the dance continuing far into the night. New couples and couples disappearing into the bushes as they form.

CATHOLIC AND INCA

THE ANDES

PILGRIM FESTIVAL
OF STARS AND SNOW

THE ANDES

PILGRIM FESTIVAL OF STARS AND SNOW

DEEP IN THE PERUVIAN ANDES, 100 KILOMETERS EAST OF THE ANCIENT INCA CAPITAL CUZCO, SOAR THE GLACIER-CAPPED SINAKARA MOUNTAINS. IN THE FOOTHILLS, SOME 15,500 (4700 M) ABOVE SEA LEVEL, IS THE COYLLUR RITTI VALLEY. HERE I PITCHED MY LITTLE TENT.

It was past 2 a.m., and very cold. From the church, a loudspeaker filled the air with the sonorous tones of a sorrowful Quechua-language hymn. The voice, without musical accompaniment, was a young woman's; her singing, simple and artless, was not always on key. And yet it throbbed with rapture and faith, enveloping in its gentle comfort the tens of thousands of pilgrims shivering in their sleep in the chill valley air. Nearly two hours had passed since the hymn-singing roused me from my shallow slumber. Eager to get back to sleep, I found instead the girl's voice penetrating deep into my consciousness. Sleep was out of the question, even apart from the commotion raised by wakeful pilgrims dancing through the night and the distant sounds of horns and countless whistles.

Without knowing a word of the Quechua language, I could nonetheless make out a name that recurs frequently in the song: "Señor de Coyllur Ritti." Coyllur means star; Ritti, snow. "Señor," in this case, is a respectful form of address to God.

Señor de Coyllur Ritti, then, refers to Jesus Christ, who once, legend has it, appeared in these mountains. The Coyllur Ritti pilgrimage, festival of stars and snow, occurs every year from late May to early June, peaking on the day of the full moon. To the stars one directs ones hopes for prosperity; the snow symbolizes good health.

This particular year (2004) the full moon fell on June 8. The day before, crosses are set up on the glacier at 16,500 ft (5000 m) above sea level. Before dawn on the 8th, hordes of pilgrims climb the mountain ice to offer prayers before carrying the crosses back down.

With a guide and his assistant, I set out from Cuzco on June 4. We spent the first night at Tinqui, a village near Coyllur Ritti, arriving at Coyllur Ritti the following day. Mawayani village, where the climb begins, was crammed with tents manned by merchants purveying provisions and miscellaneous equipment to pilgrims. From one of them I procured a horse, and we set off.

Along the way we crossed paths with a long line of people coming down – Mestizo, Native Americans and others, many of them pilgrims from Cuzco returning home the same day. There are no accommodations of any kind to be had here. One must either go home or sleep in the open, in nighttime temperatures

470 A child ukuku wearing a camouflage mask.

473 Masked dancers dance all through the night.

of -20°C. The Cuzco pilgrims, most of them, were plainly not used to mountain trekking; exhaustion was written all over their faces. The festival has grown extremely popular in recent years, said the guide; pilgrims come from as far away as Bolivia and Argentina.

The path was fairly level, and we arrived in about three hours. On the rocky slope stood a single church; in the almost excessively spacious valley was a sprawling tent village.

In 1533 the Spaniard Francisco Pizarro capped his conquest of the Inca Empire with an invasion of Cuzco, having earlier put to death Emperor Atahualpa. The Spanish pillaged and destroyed many of the temples central to Incan religion, building in their place a Catholic church, then proceeding to force Catholicism on the vanquished natives. But indigenous beliefs – in the deified sun, moon, mountains, boulders and so on – ran deep, and even at gunpoint were not easily rooted out. The Spanish accordingly resolved to create a new Catholic tradition that made allowances for the native religion.

A giant boulder at Coyllur Ritti marks the scene of a legend treasured to this day. In the foothills of these mountains lived a shepherd boy named Mayta. One day he drove his herd to Coyllur Ritti, where he met a boy dressed in rags. The boy's name was Manuel. Mayta and Manuel became close friends. Mayta shared with the hungry Manual the meat and potatoes he had brought with him.

Then it occurred to Mayta that perhaps his friend's rags could be made into new clothes. Taking a piece of the ragged cloth home with him, he talked the matter over with his father, only to learn that the cloth in question could not be woven anywhere in the vicinity of Sinakara. The father then took the strange cloth to town and showed it around. "This cloth," said the astonished priest, "clothed no ordinary person. No one but a saint could wear this."

The story eventually reached the priests and officials of Cuzco, who followed Mayta and his father to Coyllur Ritti to investigate in person. They found Manual seated on a large stone – but he had changed. The glow emanating from him dazzled the eyes of the visitors. As they timidly approached, something strange happened. Manuel vanished. On the stone where he had sat stood a wooden cross.

Mayta, overcome with grief at the loss of his friend, expired on the spot, and was buried beside the stone. The herd he had been tending promptly doubled in size, a miracle recognized as Manuel's gesture of gratitude for the kindness shown him by Mayta and his father.

The legend of Jesus' appearance at the sacred giant stone – for that is how Manuel's presence was interpreted – spread rapidly. The first pilgrimage to Coyllur Ritti took place in 1783. The present-day church incorporates the stone into its structure. On its surface is a cross, and on the cross a mournful Christ, distinctly portrayed, undergoes His Passion.

As the climactic day of the full moon approaches, the crowd of pilgrims swells daily – to 30,000 people, I'm told, though to me the crowd looked more like 70-80,000, possibly even 100,000 strong. Wave after wave of them arrived – villagers, by the look of them, of simple and deep faith, brandishing crosses and portraits of Señor de Coyllur Ritti and playing on musical instruments. One group entered the church and began to pray, not pausing even to remove the firewood, pots and pans and blankets strapped to their backs. Many villagers were moved to tears and groans of anguish by the statue, dimly illuminated by the altar candles, depicting Señor de Coyllur Ritti's Passion. Kneeling, they crossed themselves repeatedly, radiating through their tears the joy of the pilgrimage. I've witnessed any number of pilgrimages all over the world; nowhere have I seen such simple, open-hearted, passionate praying as that which I saw here. The poverty these people have endured all their lives, the hardships of life deep in the Andes, find expression in their fervent prayers. Who can see it without being touched?

They stayed up all night, dancing. The dances are of three kinds: *chuncho*, *qolla* and *runa*. The *chuncho* is a jungle dance; dancers deck their heads in bright-colored feathers. The qolla is a dance from the Lake Titicaca region. With llama dolls dangling from their waists, dancers converse imitating the llama's shrill cry. The runa is danced everywhere in the Andes – quick-tempo dance, with much cracking of whips, to the accompaniment of flutes and drums. The dancers wear knitted woolen masks and camouflage suits. As the dance reaches its climax two men move into the center of the circle and, not breaking their rhythm, lash each other about the lower body with their whips. At just the right moment a third man comes between them; the two whippers now link arms and kneel before God. The cycle is repeated over and over. The whips, of supple knitted leather, are wielded with full strength; the lashing must be intensely painful. But the men's facial expressions are invisible behind their masks, and as for cries, not so much as a peep escapes them. The whippers, called *ukukus*, are the main players in the festival. They are the guards of Señor de Coyllur Ritti.

About 165 feet (50 m) up the slope from the church, far removed in spirit from the passions of the pilgrims, an astonishing business was underway. It sells dreams to the masses. The goods for sale include replicas of houses, replicas of cars, fake diplomas from all sorts of universities, fake licenses to practice law, and so on. Business is transacted in American "dollars"; beside the replicas on display are stacks of fake American bills. For one Peruvian sol (1 sol = 29 cents) you can buy a bundle of bills "worth" $40,000. You then "contribute" this thick wad of bills to God. Who knows? Perhaps He will turn the symbolic houses and college degrees you purchased into actual material prosperity.

It's basically a form of playing house. That the players are adults, and that they are so deadly serious about it, is both funny and sad. Fake money conveying wishes to God? Long lines form; customers register their names, and deposit their fake bills in cracks in the sacred giant stone, on which candles burn. There must be hundreds of millions of fake dollars there. It's just a game, but it reveals clearly how desperate these people are to throw off the yoke of Andean poverty cramping their lives. In much the same spirit, people wait patiently in long lines at the city bank in order to cash their paltry paychecks.

Late in the afternoon of the fourth day after my arrival, my guide and I decided to climb to just beneath the glacier. The festival would reach its climax next morning before dawn, at which point swarms of pilgrims would make the climb in order to pray. My physical condition was such that I couldn't possibly keep pace with them. Having obtained a horse, I went as far as the terrain allowed on horseback. After an arduous two-hour climb, there we were, under the glacier. The altimeter showed 16,500 feet (5000 m). Frequent travel in Tibet had accustomed me to high altitudes; at this point I suffered little from them. Dusk thickened. A group of men climbing to the ice field carried crosses for the next day's ceremonies.

We spread some stones and set up our tent on a stretch of ground flat enough for us to lie down on. After a simple supper I gulped down some strong liquor and fell asleep early. What with the festive noises night after night, I hadn't slept properly since arriving in Coyllur Ritti. Tonight at least would be quiet; I should be able to sleep soundly. It was not to be, however. Maybe I was just too exhausted to sleep. In any event, I ended up lying awake through the better part of a long, miserable night.

At one point I dozed off briefly, only to be wakened by an unfamiliar sound: "Para, para . . ." It was snow beating against the tent. I looked at my watch; it was just after 3 a.m. Then I became aware of another sound, a very faint sound; it seemed to be approaching from far away. I listened intently. Unmistakably, it was the sound of flutes and horns, coming from below, gradually drawing nearer. I woke the guide, asleep beside me, and we set about preparing to be off.

Outside the tent, snow was falling in great flakes.

The path led to a ridge, from the top of which we could see in the darkness a long procession of climbers holding torches over their heads. Having ascended some 650 feet (200 m), they kept up a lively pace, horns and whistles sounding loudly within their ranks. Squinting, I could see other groups with torches making their way up the mountain to the glacier.

As they approached I saw they were all *ukukus*, their faces masked, their bodies clothed in woolen garments that made them look like bears. All were men; women were apparently prohibited from climbing on the ice. Whistles aside, they advanced in total silence, gripping a safety rope they'd formed by tying their whips together. The snow fell steadily.

To me it seemed less like a Christian service, and more like some secret ceremony in honor of local mountain gods. The natives had in fact ingeniously woven their own ancient Inca beliefs, the better to preserve them, into a Christian camouflage. Many of the mountains where crosses now stood were home to ancestral mountain gods, whose anger had to be placated with votive offerings.

An unexpected difficulty arose. Only those dressed in *ukuku* garb, we were told, were permitted to climb on the ice. It was a new rule, introduced this year for the first time. We argued the point with the leader, to no avail. Leaving us behind, the *ukukus* – they numbered several hundred – continued on their way. What could we do? The situation seemed hopeless. Just as we were about to give up, my guide spotted some people he knew among the *ukukus*. He explained the situation. Wait here, they said. They

477 Arriving at a church 4700 meters above sea level, this pilgrim, deeply moved, focuses her devotions on "Senor Coyllur Ritti."

would climb to the top, say their prayers, then return immediately and lend us the clothing we needed.

We watched and waited. Morning came. The *ukukus* swarmed round the crosses and prayed; then each one lit the candle he had brought with him and, kneeling, placed it reverently on the ice. It was no longer snowing.

Some twenty minutes later the two men we were waiting for came hurrying down toward us. I took off my down jacket and put on the *ukuku*'s colorful, rather tight poncho. Just in case I donned his mask too, and slung his whip around my neck. My camera I concealed under the poncho. Then we set off, climbing toward the crosses. Possibly because I was so tense, the cold seemed less extreme than I'd feared. Here and there on the ice were large crevasses. Around the crosses, set up in five or six places at some distance from one another, were throngs of *ukukus*.

Before the crosses, on which stood countless candles of all sizes, was a line of young people. Kneeling, they had thrust their hands into the snow. They remained in that posture for four or five minutes. At a signal from a man keeping time, *ukukus* with whips came forward and with all their strength lashed the kneeling youngsters on their buttocks. It's a kind of rite of passage. It takes place once a year during the Coyllur Ritti pilgrimage.

An hour or so later the crosses were gathered up and the pilgrims began the return trip down the mountain. Wherever you looked you saw the descending pilgrims, waving colorful flags, blowing whistles, playing on assorted musical instruments. At a certain point they met the women who, banned from climbing up the ice, had waited down below to greet the crosses. Lines formed; dancing began – vigorous, spirited dancing. I'd never seen anything like it – tens of thousands of pilgrims imploring the blessing of God, in the dead of winter, in the mountains, at 16,500 (5000 m) above sea level. It was like some majestic Andean opera.

Peru's Spanish conquerors brought Christianity with them and set about imposing it by force, but the natives, cleverly infusing it with their own ancestral beliefs, produced in the process a new, passionate, peculiarly Andean Christianity – less intolerant, more broadminded – whose influence, owing to the reach of the colonial power, in the course of time spread worldwide.

Shortly after noon, the Mass in front of the church being over, the pilgrims folded up their tents and began descending en masse, pots and pans and blankets strapped to their backs. At the head of the procession, carried carefully in a glass box, was the Coyllur Ritti statue depicting Christ's Passion. The community's protector god, it is taken once a year during the pilgrimage from the village church in which it is usually kept to the Coyllur Ritti sanctuary, in order that the people's sins of the past year may be forgiven.

479 Ukukus, spurred on by the ceaseless piping of whistles, climb across the ice through driving snow to crosses planted at the top of the mountain.

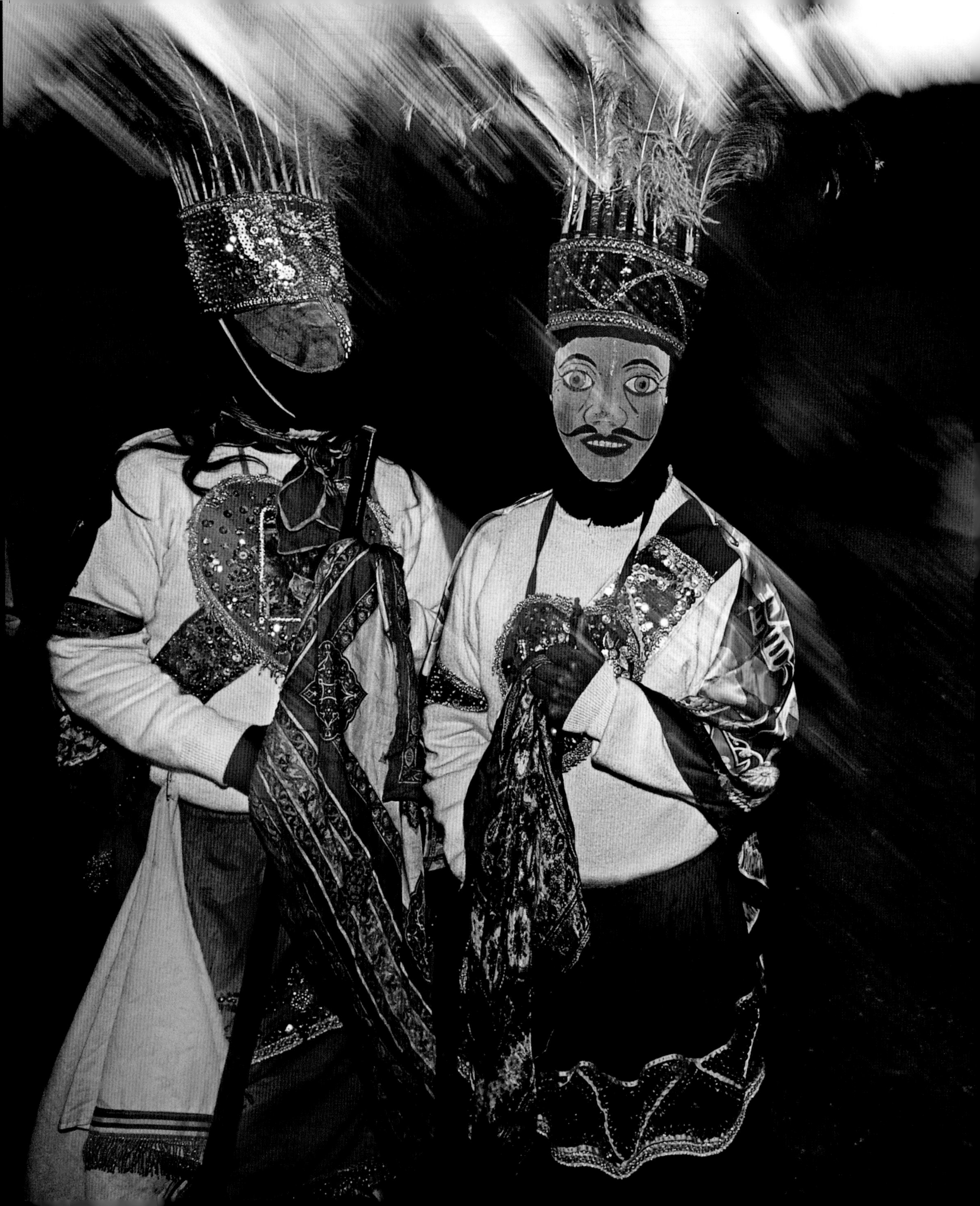

480-481 Masked dancers
are organized in hundreds
of groups depending on
the villages and towns they
come from.

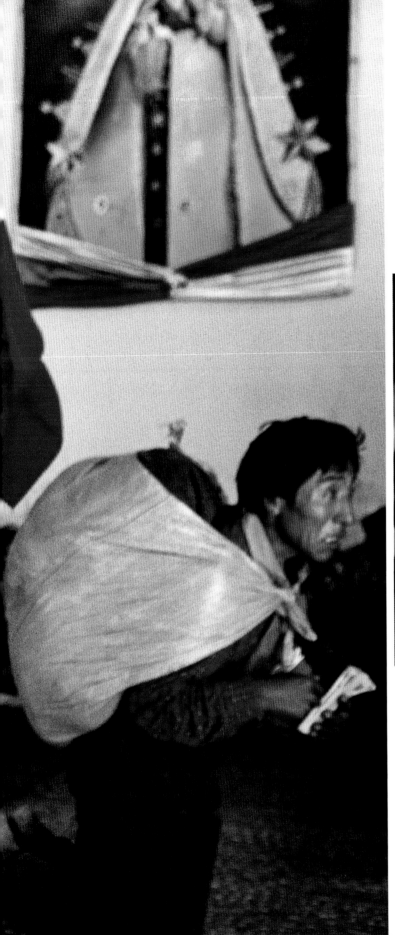

482-483 A party of villagers, arriving at the church, offer
prayers to Senor Coyllur Ritti. In the hand of the man at left
is a head ornament used in jungle dances called *chuncho*.

483 This young girl ascended the steep trail perched on
her father's shoulders.

484-485 A young man praying. Villagers
come bearing statues of Coyllur Ritti (that
is, statues depicting Christ's Passion).
Each village church has such a statue.

486 and 486-487 These villagers, bearing pots
and sleeping gear on their backs, have just
arrived. Most are moved to tears as they
contemplate the Passion of Senor Coyllur Ritti.

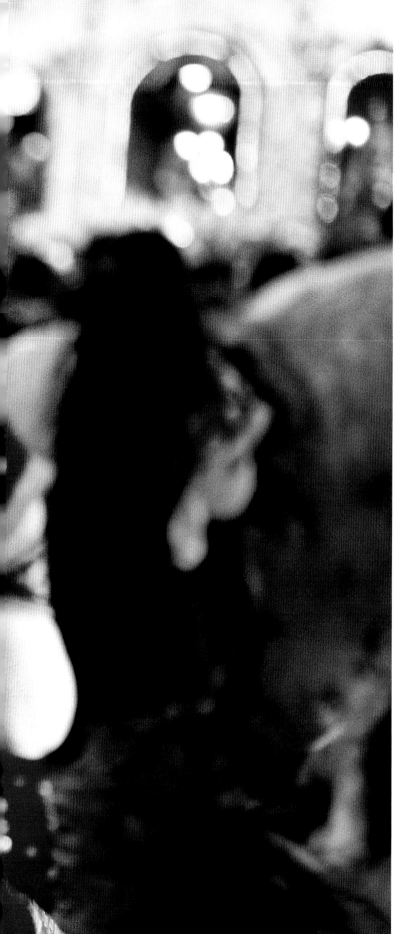

488-489 Ask whom you will about the masks worn by
ukukus, all anyone knows for sure about them is that
they are an ancient custom.

489 Dancers dressed in a costume representing the
sacred condor. Soon they will don condor masks as well.

490-491 Many of the 100,000 pilgrims
camp four days in the Coyllur Ritti Valley,
15,510 ft (4700 m) above sea level. The
church building is at right.

492 After a dance of praise to God before a sacred cavern, pilgrims kneel in prayer.

492-493 A child ukuku in a white camouflage mask known as a *huaqollo*. Children too don the characteristic weird ukuku costome, topped by a woolen tassel.

494-495 Ukukus praying at a cross
planted in the ice. Altitude: 16,500 ft
(5000 m). Each group plants tens of
crosses.

496-497 Youngsters participating in
their first festival must undergo an
initiation ceremony. Kneeling at the
cross, they plunge their bare hands in
the snow and bear it for nearly five
minutes – after which their backsides
are subjected to a ferocious whipping.

498 and 498-499 After a series of celebrations on the
ice lasting some two hours, the ukukus collect the
crosses planted the day before, and the homeward
descent begins.

500-501 A long line of ukukus descending the mountain.

K AZUYOSHI NOMACHI was born in 1946 in Kochi Prefecture, Japan. In 1971 he began his freelance career as an advertising photographer. He turned to photojournalism the following year, at age 25, in the course of his first encounter with the Sahara Desert. After two years spent photographing the desert, he followed the Nile River from delta to source and then traveled through Ethiopia, his photographs capturing Northeast Africa's harsh environment and the men and women who live in it.

From 1988 he turned his attention to Asia. Repeated trips to Tibet produced photographs depicting the religious faith and daily lives of people living at extremely high altitudes.

Converting to Islam in order to gain access to Islam's holiest cities, he traveled to Saudi Arabia at the invitation of a Saudi publisher and spent five years photographing the great annual *hajj* pilgrimage to Mecca and Medina. The photographs that resulted appeared in leading publications around the world, including National Geographic, Stern, and GEO. He has published 12 photographic anthologies in various countries. His work has won numerous prizes, among them the Annual Award of the Photographic Society of Japan in 1990 and 1997,

ACKNOWLEDGMENTS

In the course of my travels through various climates and environments around the world, many people have opened their hearts to me, giving me and my camera access to their solemn religious observances. I would like to extend to them my apologies for having at times disturbed the solemnity of their proceedings with the noise of my camera shutter. My first expression of gratitude must be for the generosity of these people of deep religious faith who graciously permitted me to photograph them. I want to express my gratitude also to the many magazine editors who have worked with me and supported me through many difficult assignments. I am grateful to Robert L. Kirschenbaum and the staff of Pacific Press Service, for building up contacts over many years with overseas publishing firms. My thanks also to master photographer Takashi Kijima, and to my family for their encouragement. For his interest in my work over 30 years, I thank Marcello Bertinetti of White Star. For taking on the huge editorial task of putting this 504-page volume together, my deepest thanks to Valeria Manferto De Fabianis, Maria Valeria Urbani Grecchi, Laura Accomazzo, Clara Zanotti and the rest of the White Star staff. My thanks also to the writer Michael Hoffman for his English translation.

504 Tibetan *ringras* – sand mandalas. A slender cone filled with sand and an empty one are rubbed together to create a vibration that allows a small, controlled amount of sand to emerge. As many as 10 priests spend four days making them. The memorial service over, the *ringras* are broken up and submerged in the river.